EDITING SIXTEENTH-CENTURY TEXTS

EDITING SIXTEENTH CENTURY TEXTS

Papers given
at the Editorial Conference
University of Toronto
October, 1965

edited by R. J. SCHOECK

PUBLISHED FOR
THE EDITORIAL CONFERENCE COMMITTEE
UNIVERSITY OF TORONTO
BY UNIVERSITY OF TORONTO PRESS

PN162
E3
1965aa

The page from the prayerbook of St. Thomas More is reproduced
with the permission of the Beinecke Library, Yale University, and
through the gracious co-operation of Professor R. S. Sylvester.

From the prayerbook of St. Thomas More, with his own marginalia made while a prisoner in the Tower, 1534–35. F6$_v$ in the Psalter of Fr. Byckman (Paris, 1522), which is bound with a Book of Hours of Fr. Regnault (Paris, 1530). The three marginalia read:

opposite Psalm 60:3 (Vulgate): diaboli
Psalm 60:7 : pro rege
Psalm 61:2 : patientia in tribulatione uel
non committam tale peccatum amplius

CONTENTS

Introduction   3
   R. J. Schoeck

Editing English Dramatic Texts   12
   S. Schoenbaum

A Note from a General Editor   24
   Clifford Leech

Editing French Lyric Poetry of the Sixteenth Century   27
   Victor E. Graham

English Translators of Erasmus 1522–1557   43
   E. J. Devereux

Three Tudor Editors of Thomas More   59
   Germain Marc'hadour

Publisher Guillaume Rouillé, Businessman and
        Humanist   72
   Natalie Zemon Davis

German Zeitung Literature in the Sixteenth Century   113
   Carl Max Kortepeter

Index   131

CONTRIBUTORS

Natalie Zemon Davis is assistant professor of economic history in the University of Toronto, having previously been assistant professor of history at Brown. Educated at Smith, Radcliffe, and Michigan (PH.D., 1959), she edits *Renaissance and Reformation*, a publication centred on Toronto libraries and scholarship.

E. J. Devereux, who taught at the University of New Brunswick before his present post at the University of Western Ontario, London, has published on lost English translations of Erasmus and on the English editions of Erasmus's *Catechismus* in *The Library*; he is a member of the Bibliographical Society (London) and the Oxford Bibliographical Society.

Victor E. Graham is professor of French in University College, University of Toronto and head of the Graduate Department of French, University of Toronto. In addition to a high-school text and two anthologies of poetry for university use, he has published, in seven volumes, the complete critical edition of the works of Philippe Desportes (1546–1606) in the series *Textes littéraires français* published by Droz.

Carl Max Kortepeter was educated at Harvard, McGill, and London (PH.D.) universities, and has taught in Turkey at Robert College and for the University of Maryland in Germany; he is at present associate professor of Islamic Studies in the University of Toronto. His study of "The Relations between the Crimean Tartars and the Ottoman Empire 1578–1608" is to be published shortly in Mouton's Central Asian Series; his essay on the fifth Lateran Council and the Turks will appear in a volume of studies on the Council being edited by R. J. Schoeck.

Clifford Leech, widely known for his judicious assessments of critical studies of Shakespeare in the *Shakespeare Survey*, for his many papers and lectures on Shakespeare and the drama, and most recently for his edition of critical essays, *Shakespeare: The Tragedies*, for the Chicago-Toronto series, Patterns of Literary Criticism, is professor of English, University College, and chairman of the Graduate Department of English, University of Toronto, as well as general editor of the Revels Plays.

Abbé Germain Marc'hadour is professor of English in the Catholic University, Angers, France. He has edited *L'Univers de Thomas More* (Vrin, 1963) and is editing More's *Supplication of Souls* for the Yale Edition of the Complete Works of St. Thomas More. He has been a fellow at both the Folger and the Huntington Libraries and is editor of *Moreana*.

R. J. Schoeck, professor of English and head of the Department of English, St. Michael's College, University of Toronto, is also a member of the Pontifical Institute of Mediaeval

Studies, Toronto. He has edited or co-edited a number of critical volumes and anthologies, is one of the editors of the Yale Edition of More, and is one of the general editors of the Chicago-Toronto Patterns of Literary Criticism series.

S. *Schoenbaum* received his PH.D. from Columbia University and is professor of English, Northwestern University. In addition to his own critical study of Middleton's tragedies and his most recent volume on *Internal Evidence and Elizabethan Dramatic Authorship* (Northwestern University Press, 1966), he has edited the revised edition of Harbage's *Annals of English Drama* and is editor of *Renaissance Drama* and *Research Opportunities in Renaissance Drama,* annual journals published by Northwestern University Press.

EDITING SIXTEENTH-CENTURY TEXTS

INTRODUCTION

R. J. Schoeck

THE CONFERENCE ON EDITORIAL PROBLEMS

Early in 1965, a group of scholars in the University of Toronto conceived the idea of a continuing conference on editorial problems at which scholars actively at work upon editorial tasks could come together for a free discussion of their work, learning from each other's experience, pooling their common intellectual resources, and seeking out expert opinion and counsel.[1] It was decided in April that the first conference would focus upon sixteenth-century editing, and the present volume presents a majority of the papers given at this conference, held on October 15 and 16, 1965, in University College and St. Michael's College of the University of Toronto, under the chairmanship of the present writer. It was a tragic shock, and a personal sadness to a number of his friends in Toronto, that the late R. C. Bald, who was to have been the first speaker, died in August, 1965; he will be greatly missed as an editor of Renaissance texts and as a bibliographer and textual scholar.

[1]Members of the committee which emerged from these discussions and plans were (during 1965): G. E. Bentley, Jr., Victor E. Graham, Peter L. Heyworth, Douglas Lochhead, J. M. Robson, R. J. Schoeck, and D. I. B. Smith.

Even though this was the first such conference, organized on rather brief notice and given little publicity, fifty-five persons attended the reception, dinner, and paper on Friday evening, and about seventy-five on Saturday. These came from as far afield as New Brunswick and St. Thomas More College, Saskatoon, in Canada; from Brown and Western Reserve in the United States; and from Angers, France, and Lagos, Nigeria. It is a pleasure to record our indebtedness to other members of the University and to all of those who made the first conference a success.

Clearly, it was fortunate that the Conference came at the time it did, for currently there is considerable editorial activity among sixteenth-century scholars: the More Edition at Yale (that home of editorial projects), the forthcoming editions of Erasmus, projected work on the Reformers, a number of series of dramatic texts, as well as considerable editing of individual dramatic and poetic texts. And we were especially pleased by the number of graduate students who came, some of them primarily interested in the period, but some in the still, to them, mysterious work of editing. The final exhortation of the first paper for the young scholar to go forth and edit was appropriate for this portion of the audience.

But, primarily, the Conference brought together scholars from diverse disciplines: English and French literatures, Near Eastern studies, history, bibliography, drama, and others; and what these scholars had in common was that they were all concerned with editorial problems of the sixteenth century. At the Conference these individuals were able to talk with each other, to compare their problems, and to cross-fertilize from experience and thinking in closely related areas which all too often are kept separate by academic boundary-lines of department or language or field.

Assured by the Dean of the Graduate School of the continuing support of the University of Toronto, the committee for the Conference on Editorial Problems is already planning a second conference, in November of 1966, to concentrate on the Nineteenth Century and a third, in 1967, on Canadian editing and publishing.

THE SATURDAY PAPERS AND DISCUSSIONS

The essays in this volume were given on Saturday morning and afternoon and have been somewhat revised, in one case substantially enlarged, for publication. What we do not represent is the other dimension of the Conference: the amount of always interesting and often valuable discussion of work and theory—with the one exception of the registering of the remarks of Professor Leech from the floor, which have been added following the paper to which they were addressed. These reflections of Professor Leech will indicate the degree of interest there was in theories and practice of modernization and normalization. There was also, during the morning session, lively discussion of the similarities and differences between the editing of dramatic and of poetic texts, and numerous comparisons of French and English editorial practices.

The chairman of the Conference from the beginning was aware of certain lacunae in his programming. Ideally, there should have been representation from scholars at work in the field of Italian publishing and engaged in editing Italian texts, even if there were no attempt at total coverage of European national literatures; no one would question the immense importance of early Italian printing or fail to recognize that valuable lessons might be learned from twentieth-century Italian editorial scholarship. The matter of classical texts—of the foundational work of the sixteenth century in editing the classics—is another lacuna. And I should have liked to see representation from the handful of brave scholars at work upon sixteenth-century legal texts: there is still much to be done

6 *Introduction*

concerning the legal printers of Tudor England, twentieth-century editing of sixteenth-century texts, and a host of other legal matters.[2] But in a day and a half of conference one could not hope to cover every facet.

What was covered, we believe, was central. The first two papers, with the additional note, firmly stress dramatic and poetic editing, and place English and French side by side, from the point of view of the modern editor, with many ideas and possibilities thrown out for the beginning scholar. Indeed, one can think of few essays that would provide sounder bearings and a firmer sense of *Methodenlehre* than Victor Graham's essay on French lyric poetry. The middle two essays, concentrating on Erasmus and More, introduce humanistic concerns, and chart some of the problems of sixteenth-century translators and editors themselves. In the final two essays, newer ground is broken, first in the study of a publisher in Lyon, with its new documentation of the economics and sociology of sixteenth-century publishing, and its intriguing material on international book trade; the final essay involving the Frankfurt Book Fair (whose twentieth-century descendant was meeting almost at the moment of our own Conference) and indicating the rôle of Eastern problems. Indeed, it is worth observing that a number of overlapping circles of aristocratic, bourgeois, and lower-class audiences and their literatures are sketched in the several papers.

[2]I have already commented on some aspects of the editing of sixteenth-century legal works in reviewing the edition of Lambarde's *Archeion* by C. H. McIlwain and Paul L. Ward (in *Speculum*, xxxiv (October, 1959), 665–7) and T. F. T. Plucknett's *Early English Legal Literature* (in *Natural Law Forum*, iv (1959), 182–90); and some suggestions for editing are given in "Canon Law in England on the Eve of the Reformation," *Mediaeval Studies*, xxv (1963), 125–147. There has been little first-rate work in English legal bibliography since the splendid work of S. E. Thorne on early editions of St. German's *Doctor and Student*, but one may now add the challenging study of Howard Jay Graham, " 'Our Tong Maternall Maruellously Amendyd and Augmentyd': The First Englishing and Printing of the Medieval Statutes at Large, 1530–1533," *UCLA Law Review*, xiii (November, 1965), 58–98.

There may well be some need to expand upon a remark from the chair concerning E. P. Goldschmidt's *Medieval Texts and their First Appearance in Print*. With some students, there has been the conclusion (entirely unwarranted by a close reading of Goldschmidt, or to anyone familiar with his bibliographical erudition) that all of the major mediaeval works had found their way into print by the end of the sixteenth century. This is, of course, not the case, and not all of the conclusions which can be drawn from the examples of English mysticism with which Goldschmidt was concerned in his book can be extended to other areas.

THE YALE EDITION OF ST. THOMAS MORE

For the Friday address on the work of the More project at Yale, and for the Saturday paper on Tudor editors of More, there was at hand the St. Michael's College copy of the 1557 English Works of More—as well as displays in a number of Toronto Libraries (University, Victoria, and St. Michael's Colleges, and the Toronto Public Library) of rare and unusual Renaissance and Reformation texts, giving example to the observation of Dr. Robert Birley that there is no visual aid "more satisfactory than a good library of old books".[3]

Formally organized in September 1958, the Yale Edition of the Works of St. Thomas More is without doubt our century's most ambitious editorial enterprise in the non-dramatic, sixteenth-century field, and the executive editor of that edition, Professor Richard S. Sylvester, was the speaker at the opening conference. His history of this project during the past eight years was instructive, even challenging, and my remarks are drawn from his Friday evening address.

[3]See *Times Literary Supplement*, November 16, 1962. Also quoted by Robert H. Taylor in his admirable address, *The Common Habitation* (privately printed, Princeton [1958]), 4.

Others have edited parts of More in the past, of course. His English works were printed by his nephew, William Rastell, in a black-letter folio of 1,500 pages in 1557, and collected volumes of his Latin works appeared under very different auspices in Switzerland and the Low Countries, in 1563 and 1565,[4] with the latter being reprinted at Frankfurt in 1689. In modern times, two editions were planned, and both abandoned. In the 1930's, Eyre and Spottiswoode launched an eight-volume edition of the English works, presenting facsimilies of the 1557 text followed by modern spelling versions. That edition, Professor Sylvester judges, was "far too lavishly planned, and obsolete, by modern standards of critical editing, even before it began to appear"; only two volumes appeared, and the edition came to a halt when the plates of Volumes 3 and 4 were destroyed in the Second World War bombing of London. Another facsimile edition was begun by F. Sullivan in 1957, but only two fascicles appeared before that edition was discontinued.

The Yale Edition, then, is the first attempt to publish all of More's extant English and Latin writings in one series, and it will embrace "almost every kind of problem that an editor of sixteenth-century materials is likely to encounter"—saving dramatic, for More's reputed dramatic compositions have been lost. Rastell's 1557 folio was at first adopted as the basic copy text, owing to the great prestige of this work, but this plan was not long followed. The editors had to give greater weight to the fact that when Rastell collected More's polemical works for printing in 1557 he gave his own early editions to the printer, and the errata sheets in those early editions, we now know, were disregarded. And, a conclusive argument against following the 1557 text, the More project at Yale "came into possession of a copy of the second edition (there were two in 1529) of More's *Supplication of Souls*, which, we were able to

[4]This point has been developed by James K. McConica, in 'The Recusant Traditions of Thomas More,' Appendix II. in *English Humanists and Reformation Politics* (Oxford: Clarendon Press, 1965).

demonstrate," Sylvester declared, "had served as printer's copy for the 1557 folio text." The principles of McKerrow, Bald, and Bowers had again been proven sound. At every step in the progress of this edition, there has been a testing of theory by practice, a planning and measuring of practice by the most enlightened and experienced theory, and none, I think, of the established textual theories have been overturned, and relatively few seriously challenged.

Consequently, early editions were used for copy texts, with full collations in the textual apparatus from the 1557 edition, and with inclusion of marginalia in the folio. This surely takes the modern reader closer to what More actually wrote. "About two-thirds of the works in the 1557 folio had been printed in More's lifetime," Sylvester commented, "and he may well have been in the print shop while some of them were going through the press."

It will be helpful to follow Prof. Sylvester's classification of the extant More materials into four categories. The first includes works extant only in manuscript and never before printed. There are some new letters, some isolated notes in manuscripts, and the Latin marginalia from More's *Book of Hours*, the prayerbook he had with him in the Tower—an exciting Yale acquisition in 1965, containing about 200 lines in More's own hand. (There are also P.R.O. materials from the Duchy of Lancaster and Chancery cases during More's years as Chancellor of these two courts, but it is not at present contemplated that these will be edited as part of the Yale edition; Professor Margaret Hastings is at work editing the Duchy of Lancaster materials.)

A second category includes English works appearing only in the 1557 folio, a slender list, featuring the *Four Last Things*, and the ninth book of the *Confutation*, and a few verses. "None of the works in the first two classes," Sylvester judges, "present any particularly difficult textual problems. In each case a solitary exemplar survives, either in manuscript or in a printed version. There are no conflicting authorities, and when cruces do occur they can be resolved only by skilful emendation."

The vast bulk of More's works are either in the third category: works extant in more than one printed edition but not in manuscript, or in the fourth: works extant in both printed editions and in manuscript. More wrote and was published during a period when manuscript and printed book overlapped, and with all of the works in category four—*Treatise on the Passion, Dialogue of Comfort,* and most of the Tower works—the editor is faced, Sylvester writes, with the "careful weighing of manuscript versions against printed editions, and the complications can be extremely daunting." But the problems are by no means solely textual, he emphasized: "once a text is firmly established and all the collations recorded, other matters cry out for attention. With the Latin works, accurate translations must be made and the difficult problems of parallel-page justification must be tackled." Introductions cover circumstances of composition, historical background, textual problems, stylistic considerations; and there must be commentary, glossary, and index.

The executive editor of the More project has had rich experience working with other editors and with the idea of "team editing" on complex works. He concluded with the observation that for work of complexity and magnitude, editorial scholarship is no longer an affair for the solitary mortal: "We work best when we work together, learning from each other's work, seeking out the expert opinion, pooling our intellectual resources, so that we can render the best possible justice to the author who is engaging our attention."

CONCLUSION

"By common consent the constitution of an author's text is the highest aim that a scholar can set before himself": this is the dictum, R. C. Bald has stressed, of a classical scholar, "and a classical scholar is far more acutely conscious than a student of the modern literatures that for over two thousand years the preservation and elucidation of the texts of the great writers has been the primary concern of literary study." To the novice, there may be an "exquisite tedium" in the work of an editor; but the experienced scholar will know that the role of an editor is always at least "the fastidious one of entremetteur," and to the dedicated the words of John Burnet above will not seem too extravagant.

The 1965 Conference began with Sylvester's "mild concluding moral" that editorial scholarship is no longer an affair for the solitary mortal, and with his earnest hope that the conference might "grow and expand into a broad co-operative effort that will make the best possible use of the human resources available to us." In different ways, the papers of the next day which are now gathered in this volume exemplify that wish; and now, assured of the continuation of the idea of such a conference, we may more firmly hope that the ideal of a co-operative effort will indeed grow and expand.

We can do no better than conclude with the words of the same John Burnet, quoted by R. C. Bald in his admirable English Institute essay:[5]

A man is led by some feeling of kinship for what is greater than himself to devote his life to the interpretation of a poet, philosopher, or historian, to the elucidation of the language itself on its purely linguistic side, or to that of the art of institutions of antiquity. Such a man will freely give himself up to the most arid and laborious investigations. No erasure in a manuscript, no half-read scholium, no fragmentary inscription will seem unworthy of his attention; no grammatical nicety or stylistic peculiarity will be passed by as too trivial for his patient study. All these things will live in his hands; for they are all transformed by his faith in something to which he can hardly give a name, but which, to him, is more real than anything else.

[5]Given to the English Institute on September 7, 1948, "Editorial Problems—A Preliminary Survey," *Studies in Bibliography* (1950), 17.

EDITING
ENGLISH DRAMATIC TEXTS

S. Schoenbaum

HE TITLE of my paper affords me remarkable leeway. While not, I trust, abusing the privilege of freedom, I shall interpret my assignment liberally enough to comment on the drama from early Tudor times until the closing of the theatres in 1642. This huge corpus of plays has been discussed, year in and year out, by the Modern Language Association conference on Research Opportunities in Renaissance Drama, a group with which I have been associated for a decade. From the first a primary concern of the scholars attending these discussions has been editions, or, rather, the want of editions, of the Elizabethan dramatists. Our speakers have been much given to wholesome exhortation, the burden of the message being: "Young scholar, go out and edit."

In 1955, when the conference got under way, discouragingly few sound texts were available. For most of the major dramatists—John Heywood and Thomas Heywood, Beaumont and Fletcher, Middleton and Massinger, Shirley, and the rest—no authoritative twentieth-century collected editions existed.

Jonson, of course, was an exception, the great Herford and Simpson edition having been brought to a triumphant conclusion in 1952. So too, in part, was Webster, despite the eccentricities of Lucas's edition of the *Complete Works*, which omits several plays in which Webster participated and includes several others in which his involvement is doubtful. Bond's *Lyly* and Collins' *Greene* are, to be sure, twentieth-century editions; but only by historical accident, not by virtue of editorial method or critical sensibility. A decade ago there was not yet on the market any multi-volume series of semi-popular editions of individual plays. Nor was there afoot even a plan for small collections, four or five plays to the volume, to replace the out-of-date Mermaids, which some of us are perhaps still inclined to view with illegitimate nostalgia as the volumes that introduced us to an astonishing body of dramatic literature. Instead, the Victorian Mermaids themselves were being reset and tricked out in modern paperback finery in order to seduce unsuspecting readers. Underneath the cosmetics they were the old Mermaids still, with all their inaccuracies preserved and some new anomalies added.[1] No doubt many have succumbed to those decrepit charms. As regards larger collections intended for the college classroom, we had to resort to the ponderous warhorses produced by a previous generation's industry: Adams's *Chief Pre-Shakespearean Dramas* (1924); Brooke and Paradise's *English Drama, 1580–1642* (1933); Hazelton Spencer's *Elizabethan Plays* (1933); Baskervill, Heltzel, and Nethercot's *Elizabethan and Stuart Plays* (1934); and last, and very much least, Parks and Beatty's *The English Drama: 900–1642* (1935). On the most advanced student level, the editing of a play to satisfy the requirements of the doctoral dissertation had not

---

[1]Thus the verso of the contents page of the original Mermaid edition of *Webster and Tourneur* provides a brief account of the Globe Theatre as an accompaniment to the frontispiece engraving. The softback edition retains the account but omits the frontispiece that justified its inclusion.

yet come into vogue at most major universities in the United States.

A decade is a significant unit of time, and a conference such as this, dedicated as it is to the consideration of editorial problems, provides a welcome opportunity to re-survey the terrain, to take stock of advances made, to record disappointment with prophecies still unfulfilled, and to confront once again some of the stubborn problems that are our challenge and sometimes our despair.

It is pleasant to be able to say straightaway that some striking headway has been made, especially with regard to editions of individual works. In 1958 the Revels Plays series, under the general editorship of Clifford Leech, was auspiciously launched with N. W. Bawcutt's excellent edition of Middleton and Rowley's *The Changeling*; since then volumes have appeared at the rate of about one a year. There can be no doubt that this series, which provides editions roughly analogous in scope to the New Arden *Shakespeare*, has found its niche. (On some of the problems presented by these and other modern-spelling texts, I shall have occasion to remark later; for the moment I am concerned simply with the fundamental matter of the availability of the plays in editions of any kind.) During the crucial initial stages of the series the general editor kept, no doubt wisely, to the tried and true. Titles thus far published include *The Spanish Tragedy*, *Dr. Faustus*, and Webster's two great tragedies; the rest, with the exception of Tourneur's *The Atheist's Tragedy*, are equally familiar and accessible plays. But we have been promised in future "certain lesser-known plays which remain in general neglect despite the lively interest that an acquaintance with them can arouse." R. A. Ffoakes's keenly-awaited edition of *The Revenger's Tragedy* is scheduled soon to appear. Middleton's *A Chaste Maid in Cheapside* and *Women Beware Women*, as well as others, are in preparation. Thus this important series has begun to acknowledge shifts in sensibility that have brought about a revaluation of plays in the past comparatively neglected. The three titles I have just mentioned are not included in any of the large anthologies of Elizabethan plays; yet specialists recognize them as among the major dramas of the age. The Revels Plays will now perform the important service of introducing them to the larger class of readers, many of them students, to whom a semi-popular edition caters. One hopes that this kind of service will be maintained and extended as the series progresses.

Launched as recently as 1963, the Regents Renaissance Drama Series, under the general editorship of Cyrus Hoy, has already almost a score of titles to its credit, with many more to follow. Textually these editions resemble the Revels Plays in that they are in modern spelling and based upon fresh collations of the early quartos; but introductory matter and annotation are less elaborate. From the first, the selection of plays for editing has been adventurous. One particularly welcomes the new editions of Middleton's *A Mad World, My Masters* and Marston's *Antonio and Mellida, Antonio's Revenge,* and *The Dutch Courtesan.* A great many other titles have been commissioned for this flourishing series. It is good to be able to look forward to such comparative novelties as Lyly's *Mother Bombie,* Porter's *Two Angry Women of Abingdon,* and Shirley's *The Court Secret.*

The latest multi-volume series to enter the lists is the New Mermaid project under the supervision of Philip Brockbank of the University of York. These editions are on approximately the same scale as the Regents; they are similar in format, and retail at about the same price. Of the seventeen plays I have seen announced for the New Mermaids, all but two (Greene's *James IV* and the readily available *New Way to Pay Old Debts* by Massinger) are also on the Regents list. This situation presents a novel problem. For years we had to endure dearth; the cries of hungry students went unheeded. Now we are confronted with the ills of affluence and must reckon with the inconveniences of surfeit. Traps await the unwary. The technical demands made upon contributors to the New Mermaids are not equivalent to those which Hoy, trained in the hard school of Bowers, has set for his Regents editors. Yet *The Times Literary Supplement* reviewer, commenting on the nearly simultaneous publication of *The City Madam* and *Bussy D'Ambois* in the two series, regards these editions as equally suitable for student consumption. If the professional judge thus falters in his task, what may we expect of the inexperienced undergraduate? I suppose what I am asking for is greater vigilance from the specialist and a willingness on his part to undertake serious reviews of mere paperbacks.

Pointless duplication is another problem. Surely it is wasteful of effort to have three scholars subject themselves to the exquisite tedium of collating the sixteenth- and seventeenth-century quartos of the same play for three different series. And surely it is wasteful of opportunity for the publishers of the same series to place the same plays on the market. No doubt the competitive conditions that prevail in the industry conspire to make a certain degree of waste inevitable, and I suppose ultimately the superior series will drive out the inferior. But I wonder whether some of the overlapping is not simply the result of ignorance: I wonder whether Ernest Benn in London knows what the University of Nebraska Press in Lincoln is up to, and vice versa. If these dark suspicions have some foundation, perhaps conferences such as this one and the Modern Language Association group may perform a useful function by voicing our concern and by including the publishers in our mailing lists for conference reports and surveys of works in progress.[2]

[2]A similar concern has just been expressed on the other side of the Atlantic by Ian Donaldson in *Essays in Criticism*, XV (October, 1965): ". . . it will be serious if duplication continues at the same frequency, and results in a situation where we have (say) several editions of *Bussy D'Ambois*, with perhaps little to choose between them, and still no cheap edition giving us five or six of Chapman's plays" (454).

When we turn from editions of individual plays to collections of several or more pieces, we move from lush vegetation to dry and rocky soil: so little is there that merits report. An exception is the Curtain Playwrights project which recently produced its first volume, *Shakespeare in Seventeenth-Century Germany*, under the general editorship of the late R. C. Bald. It is to be hoped that a successor will be found to carry on the work of the distinguished scholar who planned the series and commissioned for it several volumes of English Renaissance plays.

So far as larger collections are concerned, the picture is gloomy indeed. The past decade has produced no new anthology with selections made in accordance with modern critical preferences and with texts edited in conformity with modern bibliographical techniques. For the pre-Shakespearean drama we must still resort to the Adams collection, notable for its bowdlerized texts, inanely superfluous stage directions, and generally inadequate introductions and notes. Although as a matter of practical necessity I have had to exclude recent editions of Shakespeare from this survey, I may perhaps depart momentarily from my self-imposed limitation to refer to a striking, if depressing fact. The two most popular one-volume complete *Shakespeare*'s prescribed for undergraduate use in the United States faithfully follow the Globe edition of 1864, as though the century of scholarly investigation during which a bibliographical revolution took place had in no way significantly contributed to our knowledge of Shakespeare's text! An editorial deficiency of such magnitude does not pass unnoticed; other speakers have properly deplored the situation at similar scholarly gatherings. That we have had to struggle along with relics of the past is humanly understandable considering that the technical demands made on the editor by modern textual scholarship effectually inhibit ambition.

Yet our needs remain. They will not be satisfied by the updating of an outmoded collection, as Robert Ornstein has

recently attempted to do in his two volumes of Elizabethan
and Jacobean comedies and tragedies, based upon the old
Hazelton Spencer anthology. Ornstein's critical introductions
have the sophistication to be expected of the gifted author of
The Moral Vision of Jacobean Tragedy, but the texts themselves, as well as the annotations, are mere reprints of Spencer.
The result is a hodge-podge of old and new. In textual scholarship, if not necessarily in human affairs, marriages of convenience seldom succeed. The alternative is to start from
scratch, as Irving Ribner and Richard Hosley, highly qualified
scholars both, are doing with their anthology which is now
in preparation. Another possibility is to bring together within
the covers of a single volume the individual plays of a multi-
volume series, as Cyrus Hoy has in mind for the Regents
undertaking, and (I believe) Alfred Harbage for the Pelican
Shakespeare.

The most signal achievement of editing in our field is,
of course, the authoritative edition of a writer's entire *œuvre*.
In this line much has been promised and little, thus far,
delivered. The fourth and final volume of the Bowers *Dekker*,
which will serve as a model for prospective editors, appeared
in 1961. The edition as it now stands is limited to texts and
textual introductions but will eventually be supplemented by
a volume of commentary which Professor Hoy has in hand.
Announced as in preparation are Beaumont and Fletcher,
Chapman, Greene, Thomas Heywood, Lyly, Marlowe, Marston, Massinger, Middleton, and others. Some of these editions
have already been in the works for many years. The slow
progress is not surprising in view of the magnitude of the
editorial task presented by these dramatists, many of whom
were discouragingly prolific. In the old days a gentlemanly
and learned connoisseur of the old drama such as A. H.
Bullen could unaided turn out half a dozen massive collections
in as many years. But Bullen is a pre-revolutionary figure. He

did not see himself as having to establish a text, and so did not have to worry about compositors and collations. Instead he depended upon the pioneer efforts of his predecessors. "It is hardly necessary to say," Bullen writes in the preface to his *Peele,* "that I have availed myself to the fullest extent of Dyce's labours."[3] He makes similar acknowledgments in his *Middleton* and elsewhere. With reference to Marston, whom he edited in three volumes, Bullen remarks: ". . . I have done my best to regulate the text, which is frequently very corrupt; but I am painfully conscious that I have left plenty of work for future editors."[4] No responsible editor today could take so casual a view of his duties. Consequently we must patiently bide our time, and be grateful meanwhile to the university presses which agreed to sponsor these expensive undertakings and which must also patiently bide their time. Perhaps I will be permitted to express the hope that, while waiting, we might look forward also to a new John Heywood (among the earlier dramatists) and a new James Shirley (of the very late ones). Heywood has never been seriously edited; critics still depend on the Farmer reprint which is an abomination. A major Caroline dramatist, Shirley has not been edited since 1833, when Dyce brought to completion and published the edition begun by Gifford.

While on individual playwrights, I must not neglect to mention Ribner's recent edition of *The Complete Plays of Christopher Marlowe,* designed for "the modern student and the general reader." It is an attractive volume that deserves the warm reception it has had from reviewers. Ribner has evidently taken his work seriously, for "each of the plays has been freshly edited from the early text which is demonstrably most authoritative." Yet this edition raises in rather striking fashion an important question that has not, to my mind, been

---

[3]*The Works of George Peele* (London, 1888), I, pref., ix.
[4]*The Works of John Marston* (London, 1887), I, pref., vii.

thoroughly enough aired. In his critical introduction Ribner argues forcefully and at some length for what can only be regarded as a highly controversial interpretation of *Faustus*:

. . . Marlowe's *Doctor Faustus* is not a Christian morality play because it contains no affirmation of the goodness or justice of the religious system it portrays. It is, rather, a protest against this system, which it reveals as imposing a limitation upon the aspirations of man, holding him in subjection and bondage, denying him at last even the comfort of Christ's blood, and dooming him to the most terrible destruction.[5]

I have strong reservations about this reading, which seems to me dangerously to oversimplify the rich ambivalences of Marlowe's thought and the rich ambiguities of his dramatic technique. Controversial interpretations appear elsewhere in Ribner's introduction. He is entitled to his views: the question I would ask is whether he or any editor is justified in making an edition intended for the student or general reader a vehicle for partisan interpretive criticism.

The *raison d'être*, as I see it, of such an edition is to provide a sound text and such aids to the understanding as glosses for difficult, obscure, or archaic words and phrases. When the editor proceeds beyond these limited objectives to indulge in fancy criticism, is he not in effect having a free ride at the expense of a captive audience that has paid its money for the plays? Many students and ordinary readers will have neither the critical discernment nor the necessary background to evaluate judiciously the interpretations provided them; instead they will yield to the magical potency of the printed word. I must confess to some bias in favour of the plan of Tucker Brooke's edition of *The Works of Christopher Marlowe*, first printed in 1910 and designed, like Ribner's, "to furnish the student and the general reader with a serviceable edition of Marlowe's accepted writings." Brooke limits his introductory matter to brief remarks on such matters as dates of composition,

[5]Introd., xxxvii.

early editions and stage history, authorship, and sources.[6] I
realize that some of the views I have just expressed on the role
of the editor are, to say the least, debatable. I realize too that
someone who agrees to do a play for a series—say, the Regents
or the new Arden—must accommodate himself to the general
pattern of that series. He need not, on the other hand, use
the interpretive sections of his introduction for special plead-
ing; an objection that may fairly be raised against Richard
David's new Arden edition of *Love's Labour's Lost*. On the
general question I have submitted I would be most interested
to hear the opinions of other members of this conference.

Brooke's *Marlowe* is an old-spelling edition, whereas Ribner
chooses to modernize. The relative merits of old- *versus*
modern-spelling is a perennial problem that has often been
discussed at professional meetings. It is also fundamental, and
therefore I do not propose to pass over it in silence today,
although the limited time left at my disposal will not permit
me to say very much. In recent editorial practice a clear pattern is discernible. Old-spelling is of course *de rigueur* for
editions (like the Bowers *Dekker*) prepared with fellow specialists in mind. Most semi-popular editions—by which I mean
editions intended mainly for university undergraduates—offer
modernized texts. This is the case with the Revels Plays, the
Regents Renaissance Drama Series, the New Mermaids, and
all recent editions of Shakespeare. The only exception I know
of—an interesting one—is the Anchor Seventeenth-Century
Series, under the editorial guidance of J. Max Patrick, which
includes two unhackneyed small collections of Jacobean plays
edited by Richard Harrier.

[6]These remarks are not intended to imply a preference for Tucker
Brooke's *Marlowe* over Ribner's for classroom use. The Brooke edition,
admirable for its day, is textually outmoded; the editor's decision to follow
the 1604 quarto of *Doctor Faustus*, "relegating to an Appendix the probably
spurious additions and revisions of 1616" (p. 141), is by itself sufficient to
disqualify the text from serious consideration by the present generation of
students, who are in a position to profit from Greg's classic work on
Faustus.

The most powerful argument for modernization, so far as I am able to see, stems from concern for the unspecialized reader's convenience. This reader has enough trouble (so the argument runs) coping with the plays themselves, without the added burden—or should I say *burthen*—of old spelling. Also, by imparting a quaint look to the text, such spelling widens the gap between the modern reader and the literature of an earlier age. The main objection to modern spelling is (very roughly) that it creates problems for the editor; problems which have consequences for the reader. For the editor must make some compromises with the old spelling he is rejecting. In practice he will retain archaic forms for the sake of metre or rhyme or to preserve a meaning that would otherwise be lost. Thus the editor is faced continually with decisions about whether or not modernize a particular word. If an archaic form—*murther*, for example, or *lanthorn*—is needed in one place for the sake of rhyme or a pun, does consistency require the editor to retain the same forms if they occur elsewhere in the same text without affecting rhyme or meaning? ". . . where the copy text decrees," declares Hoy, "the Regents editions read 'thorough' and not 'through,' 'venter' and not 'venture,' 'cleves' and not 'cliffs' (as in i. 59 of *Friar Bacon and Friar Bungay*), 'bankrout' and not 'bankrupt.'"[7] But what if *venter* and *venture* both appear in the same text? Because in the sixteenth and earlier seventeenth centuries the apostrophe before final *s* was not yet in general use, an editor must often decide between singular and plural, and sometimes between an ordinary plural and a contraction with *is*. Thus in the second Gower chorus in *Pericles*, *troubles* ("in troubles raigne," I. vii) can be understood as an ordinary plural noun or as a possessive singular (Malone's reading). The modern editor prefers *troubles*. In such cases he cannot always be sure that his decision is the

---

[7]"The Regents Renaisance Drama Series," *Research Opportunities in Renaissance Drama*, VIII (1965), 10–11.

right one, for either reading may fit the context.[8] An old-spelling text, by preserving the original forms, allows the reader to grapple with legitimate alternative interpretations. That is, or should be, one of the reader's prerogatives. The deliberately archaic atmosphere of *Pericles* makes for special problems for the editor who must modernize,[9] and other plays of course present their own individual difficulties.

As you may gather from the drift of these remarks, I think there is much to be said in behalf of old-spelling texts, even in the undergraduate classroom. Surely the illusion of quaintness fades very quickly as the reader settles down to the material at hand. Surely, too, we underestimate the calibre of the present generation of undergraduates when we assume that old-spelling texts will be a trauma for them. Most of these students will be upperclassmen and English majors. In other courses they will be asked to read Chaucer and Spenser in the original. They will tackle willingly, even with eagerness, difficult modern works like *The Waste Land, Ulysses*, or *The Sound and the Fury*. Why not old spelling?

The last point I will be able to touch on is the editing of plays to meet the PH.D. dissertation requirement. Last year I published a checklist, intended for prospective editors, of plays, masques, etc., for the period 1552–1659. The list consisted of 316 items that had never been edited, and 220 not edited since 1900. Some of the entries admittedly are the merest fragments. A large number are Latin plays, the editing of which requires a skill in language that many graduate students these days regrettably no longer possess. There nevertheless remains, after all the exclusions, a very substantial number of plays that are of interest for aesthetic, historical, or

[8]For further illustration of this problem and others presented by modernization, see Arthur Brown's excellent paper, "Editorial Problems in Shakespeare: Semi-Popular Editions," *Studies in Bibliography*, VIII (1956), 15–26.

[9]See F. D. Hoeniger's introduction to the new Arden edition (London, 1963), xlix–l.

textual reasons, or for a combination of all three. Editions of these plays would be, I feel, excellent dissertation projects. I suppose one still occasionally hears a colleague, nourished in other pastures, assert that editing is hackwork to be undertaken, if at all, by the more pedestrian spirits; but that attitude is happily vanishing. I have also heard it said, by one of our most eminent bibliographers, that the editing of a text is the apex of scholarly achievement and therefore no fit teething ring for a callow graduate student. But is literary criticism any better suited for the cutting of teeth? Or is the history of ideas? If we account the undertaking, in these circumstances, a high-level exercise and reserve it for pupils who are apt and toward, it will confer benefits rather than do harm. With such students in mind, I can conclude with a familiar exhortation: Young scholar, go out and edit.

A NOTE FROM A GENERAL EDITOR

In saluting Professor Schoenbaum's admirable paper on "Editing English Dramatic Texts," I may be permitted to comment briefly on three points he raises.

(1) He draws attention to the duplication of titles in some of the series of Elizabethan and Jacobean plays that are now on the market. Here first of all it may be observed that these series are not all of the same scope. As one who has been concerned in the Revels Plays, I should like to say how much I welcome, for example, the Regents series with its high standards and attractive appearance. In the Revels we are producing our volumes much more slowly, because we are putting heavier demands on our editors; and we cannot hope for so wide a circulation. But where two series are of similar scope, there is surely a need for the respective General Editors to keep in touch and to avoid unnecessary duplication. We cannot expect the publishers to do it, for they are likely to want to include the plays with the most established reputations. At the same time, a General Editor may well feel

he is justified in including a play done elsewhere if the edition planned for his series is in some way notably different from that in the other series.

I may add that recently, as General Editor of the Revels, I conferred with one of the General Editors of the Yale Jonson before deciding to include another Jonson play in our series. Only when I knew that they had no plans involving this particular play did I decide to go ahead.

(2) A word should be said in favour of modern-spelling editions of Elizabethan and Jacobean plays, because Professor Schoenbaum has expertly referred to some of the difficulties entailed. There are indeed two things I should like to mention. First, whatever view we take of the matter, our students are going to read Shakespeare in modern spelling, and if we offer them Jonson and Webster and Chapman and Marlowe in old spelling, we are immediately suggesting that Shakespeare is still "contemporary" and they are buried in an antique mist. For his sake and for theirs, we need to get this mist out of the way. All the dramatists of the time were working in similar circumstances: Shakespeare was, of course, the supreme one, but they were his fellows, occasionally even his near-rivals, and he will be understood better if seen in their context. That can be effected only if they appear in the same form as he does. Secondly, we want our texts to be used in the theatre, and they will not be so used if they are in old spelling. The surest way to bring the old Mermaids back into currency would be for our new editions to abandon the practice of modernization. We want the plays to be read, by graduates and by undergraduates and by "general readers" too, but at least as much we want the plays acted, and we want good texts to be the basis for acting.

(3) Professor Schoenbaum has asked our editors to abstain from partisan critical opinion. And rightly he reminds us of the editor's duty to indicate the consensus of opinion on the interpretation of his play. But too many editors merely give the consensus, particularly the immediately fashionable consensus. Let an editor quote Elyot and *The French Academie* and the *Mirror for Magistrates*: most reviewers will greet him as sound, even if what he has done is to reduce his play to the level of the general thinking of the age. Dramatists are often eccentric people, particularly if they are good dramatists. A satisfactory interpretation of their work demands a special sensitiveness to an individual's variation

upon current thinking. In some cases—one thinks especially of Marlowe and Chapman—the variation from the norm can be fairly extreme. So I would urge that we encourage our editors to be independent while at the same time demanding from them that they carefully indicate where they differ from received opinion or whether there is a body of opinion at least as current as the one they are giving emphasis to. A critical introduction should not be merely what the informed reader will expect: it is good to take the reader by surprise; an edition can be a work of pioneering criticism, and, if it blazes a false trail, that will not matter if the editor admits where he has left the caravan. Let us not demand that he be dull.

CLIFFORD LEECH

EDITOR: 1. [Especially in editorial work upon texts of earlier periods, where language and dialect and other concerns enter, normalization may take on other overtones and colourations. Bald has acutely observed that there is "a real difference between normalization and the expansion of contractions, or the attempt to reproduce in type scribal peculiarities outside the range of the printer's case. The value of the facsimile reprint, in other words, is strictly limited, and photographic aids are diminishing its usefulness. Hence, as a literary student—as distinct from the historian or the paleographer—I deplore the over-meticulous habit of printing legal records and other old documents with all their contractions expanded in italics. The silent expansion of contractions is but a courtesy to the reader. Actually, many of these documents ought merely to be described and summarized, with a few of the important phrases quoted; the class of document to which the example belongs may be indicated, if necessary, through reference to historical source books or to formularies." ("Editorial Problems," p. 17.)]
2. [For a differing point of view, see the argument of Fredson Bowers on "Principle and Practice in the Editing of Early Dramatic Texts," in *Textual and Literary Criticism* (Cambridge: The University Press, 1959), 117–150.]
3. [Compare the statement of Cyrus Hoy on the Regents Renaissance Drama Series in *Research Opportunities in Renaissance Drama*, viii (1965), 10–14, with its singling out of R. J. Lordi's handling of punctuation in the editing of Chapman's *Bussy d'Ambois*.]

R.J.S.

EDITING
FRENCH LYRIC POETRY
OF THE SIXTEENTH CENTURY

Victor E. Graham

HE ROLE of editor is always a fastidious one and never more so than in the context of sixteenth-century French lyric poetry. Here a poet, inevitably *ondoyant et divers,* must be presented by the discreet *entremetteur* to a hypothetical reader equally capricious in his tastes. It is the editor's task to choose the basic garb in which his protégé will appear but near at hand he must also keep ready a great assortment of interchangeable accessories which may be demanded by the discriminating client.

In contrast to dramatic texts where the quest seems always to be to restore the one authentic original costume, there is no general agreement as to which of many lyrical garments is the most appropriate. Some insist on the first as being the most natural and unaffected; others prefer the last, where little imperfections of execution have presumably been eliminated; still others would have some intermediate one, a favourite, probably, because it was the first dress in which they saw the fickle muse. At any rate the editor must provide the means whereby any one of these evolving costumes may be quickly reconstructed for the delectation of a sophisticated patron. And he must in every instance proceed on the assumption that many of the sartorial refinements which he has catalogued will be of interest to others in ways of which he himself may not be aware.

The first prerequisite in any serious editorial project is, of course, to find out as much as you can about your poet and that is why so many important critical editions have been preceded by biographical and bibliographical studies. Henri Chamard, the editor of Du Bellay, and Paul Laumonier, the great authority on Ronsard, each began with doctoral theses on the life and works of their poets.

All such documentation is extremely important but there is also a very real danger in spending too long on preliminaries where the ramifications are infinite; one risks never starting or at least never finishing the definitive critical edition which was the ultimate objective. Laumonier died before his edition was completed but he was more fortunate than most editors because others have carried on the work which he began even though the project is still incomplete some fifty years after the appearance of the first volume. The occupational disease which threatens so many scholar-editors is not myopia as might be supposed but rather an affliction much more insidious and much more incapacitating—presbyopia!

My own experience in editing lyric poetry began with the secular works of Philippe Desportes who succeeded Ronsard as official poet to the court of France in 1575. Fortunately for me a French scholar named Jacques Lavaud had already spent nearly fifteen years preparing a *doctorat d'état* on Desportes which included, in addition to the usual biographical material, a bibliography of his works, and an analysis of certain characteristic features of his poetry.[1] As his *thèse com-*

---

[1]Jacques Lavaud, *Un poète de cour au temps des derniers Valois, Philippe Desportes* (1546–1606), (Paris: Droz, 1936).

plémentaire he presented a critical edition of the very first of Desportes's publications, the relatively unimportant imitations of Ariosto—*Les Imitations de l'Arioste*.[2] Not long after the publication of these two volumes, early in 1936, Lavaud became a dean and, needless to say, soon abandoned the idea of completing the critical edition which he had originally hoped to publish. When in 1950 I had the temerity to suggest that I would like to follow in his footsteps, he gallantly gave me his blessing and even though my edition no doubt lacks the historical and literary annotations which would have enriched it had it been completed by the original biographer of Desportes, it is at least a complete unit, and the ten years of intermittent labours which it represents could certainly never have been spared by the man best qualified for the job.[3]

In undertaking a project which was more ambitious than I realized, I was much encouraged by two remarks which I read in *Les Techniques de la critique* by Gustave Rudler, a book which still stands as a most reliable editorial guide despite the fact that it was published in 1923.[4] In speaking of the well-trod paths of scholarship which every novice finds wherever he turns, Rudler had this word of encouragement to offer: "Tout n'est pas dit, et il ne faut pas trop se laisser intimider par l'autorité des maîtres. Ils sont faillibles."[5] At the same time he offers this word of caution which the budding editor must also remember if he is ever to finish the

---

[2]Jacques Lavaud, ed., *Les Imitations de l'Arioste par Philippe Desportes, suivies de poésies inédites ou non-recueillies du même auteur* (Paris: Droz, 1936).

[3]The complete edition consists of seven volumes in the series *Textes littéraires français* published by Droz in Geneva: No. 78, *Cartels et Masquarades, Épitaphes* (1958); No. 85, *Les Amours de Diane* I and No. 86, *Les Amours de Diane* II (1959); No. 93, *Les Amours d'Hippolyte* (1960); No. 97, *Les Elégies* (1961); No. 98, *Cléonice, Dernières Amours* (1962) and No. 101, *Diverses Amours* (1963).

[4]Gustave Rudler, *Les Techniques de la critique et de l'histoire littéraires en littérature française moderne* (Oxford: The University Press, 1923).

[5]*Ibid.*, 1.

task in hand: "Mais tout n'est plus à dire. Il ne faut pas tout suspecter, tout recommencer. . . . Il faut tenir le milieu entre un respect idolâtre et une défiance universelle."[6]

With this advice in mind I began first to examine the bibliography of the works of Desportes, and if I in turn might offer a word of advice it would be this: Be sure that your bibliography is as complete as you can make it before you start the practical business of collating and then proceed chronologically even though it may mean that you have to wait for microfilms or travel considerable distances in order not to break the sequence. To deal first with the material at hand, as I did, is to add greatly to the effort ultimately involved.

As far as Lavaud's bibliography was concerned, I soon found that it was exhaustive for France but not for other sources which he had apparently overlooked. The hunt for manuscripts and editions is, to a certain extent, never-ending and I suppose it is only natural for French scholars to assume that most of their material is to be found in France. In this case, however, this was not a valid assumption and a great many items turned up in England, Canada, and the United States.[7] There may well be others in Italy, Germany, Poland, and Russia but I was not able to carry my own search that far and for the study of Desportes there would really be little interest in doing so. Between 1573, which is the date of the first edition of *Les Premieres œuvres*, and 1606 when the poet died—a period of some thirty-three years—there are about thirty known editions of his works, not to mention early manuscripts of various kinds. In general, the variants are stylistic and cumulative and the discovery of one or two more

---

[6]*Ibid.*, 2.
[7]These were listed in the following article: "Supplément à la bibliographie des œuvres de Desportes," *Bibliothèque d'humanisme et renaissance*, XIX (1957), 485–8.

unknown editions could scarcely add much to our knowledge of Desportes.

For the United States my main source of information was, of course, the National Union Catalogue in Washington and here I think I first learned to distrust the overweening authority of institutional listings. I discovered, for instance, that some items in the Union Catalogue were incorrect; afterwards, having been put on my guard, I wrote to all the most likely American university libraries and found that a fair number of them possessed editions of Desportes which somehow had not found their way into the Union Catalogue at all.

It was about this time also that I learned how useful academic gossip can be. After my preliminary letter of inquiry to Jacques Lavaud I then with some trepidation wrote to a number of internationally prominent *seiziémistes* in order to try to make sure that no one else was engaged on the same project. I was gratified and proud to receive sympathetic and helpful replies from these eminences, and later on, when I was able to meet some of them, I was astonished to discover that they were quite human and even predisposed to be interested in anyone working in a field less intensively tilled than most.

In the meantime I had also discussed the idea of such an edition with all those of my colleagues who would listen to me and soon, from a variety of people, I began to receive clippings taken out of second-hand booksellers' catalogues and notes with significant references in books which might not otherwise have come to my attention. One item which was of particular interest was a catalogue which listed for sale a copy of the 1587 version of *Les Amours de Diane* which had been privately printed in Lyon in 1928 by Hugues Vaganay, librarian-in-chief of that city. I immediately ordered this book and on receiving it read in the introduction the following intriguing passage where Vaganay explained how he had come to dedicate the volume to the memory of René Sturel, a promising young scholar who had been killed in the First Great War. He wrote in part:

Ce jeune érudit, prématurément ravi à la science et à ses amis ne se promettait pas moins que d'étudier et de publier les nombreuses "variae lectiones" des œuvres de Desportes antérieures à la première édition de 1573 et nous devions ensemble compléter ce premier travail indispensable par l'édition de 1607 accompagnée de toutes les variantes de 1573 à cette date.[8]

Vaganay himself had died in 1936 but there were indications that the work had been started so the next step was to write to the public library in Lyon to see if any· of this material could be located. Again scholarly courtesy manifested itself and the then librarian, who could find no trace of any papers dealing with Desportes, suggested that I write to Vaganay's son whose address he enclosed. This I did and, knowing that his father had been a collector, I also inquired incidentally if by chance he was in possession of any of the extremely rare sixteenth-century editions of Desportes.

The reply concerning the collated material was negative but Monsieur Vaganay, *fils*, went on to say that his father's library, which he had inherited, did in fact contain some twenty editions of Desportes including all the most important ones, any of which he would be willing to sell if I were interested. I suppose that this was for me the most exciting moment in this particular project and one brought about, as so often happens, quite by chance. The lesson, which is a valid one, is that no lead should be overlooked, however tenuous it may seem. There are always discoveries waiting to be made, and very often making a discovery is just as simple as knowing where to look.

[8]*Les Amours de Diane par Philippe Desportes*: Texte de 1587, précédé d'une introduction par Hugues Vaganay (Mâcon: Protat frères; Lyon: Hugues Vaganay, 3 rue Auguste Comte, 1928), 3.

Among the volumes which I decided to purchase for my own use was a first edition published in Paris in 1573 by Robert Estienne, one of only eight extant copies, which was very modestly priced because several pages were missing from the table of contents, a lacuna which did not in any way affect the text. Others were the collected editions of 1583, 1587, and 1600, the latter perhaps the most significant of all Desportes's editions because of the Malherbe commentary which is based on it.

Those interested in the evolution of French classicism will know of the importance of Malherbe whose ideas on language and style are to be found mainly in an annotated copy of the 1600 edition of the works of Desportes now in the *Bibliothèque Nationale* in Paris. This commentary had been transcribed by Lalanne in his edition of the works of Malherbe but he had given no indication of words crossed out, underlined, or bracketed for one reason or another by the crotchety pedant. Because of the double interest in Desportes and Malherbe it seemed indispensable to publish this commentary in its entirety and therefore to utilize as the basic text a late edition of the works of Desportes rather than the first one.

Desportes, like so many of his contemporaries, constantly revised his poetry for each successive edition of his works, sometimes replacing a word or two but more often altering whole blocks of verse with the result that many of his poems are so changed over a period of years that they are scarcely recognizable. He also was in the habit of modifying the sequence of his poems and one sometimes wonders whether all this was not done, in part, to encourage sales since each new edition bore the title *Les Premieres œuvres* or *Les Œuvres* "*reveües, corrigées, et augmentées outre les precedentes impressions.*" In any case the agglomeration of variants is extremely complex and unwieldy and the text of the early editions is often quite remote from that criticized by Malherbe.

When we come to 1600, however, we find that Desportes was by then rather more preoccupied with completing his rhymed translations of the Psalms of David than with continuing to rework his secular poetry. After the turn of the century the only revised edition of his works which the poet seems to have authorized is the one which appeared in 1607, the year following his death. It bears the exceptional title *"Derniere édition reveüe et augmentée par l'Auteur."* The modifications introduced at this time affect only some 150 lines and since they are all quite characteristic of Desportes, one may be certain that they are indeed genuine.

My selection of a basic text could be reduced then to a choice between the 1600 edition annotated by Malherbe and the 1607 edition with final emendations by the poet himself. Influenced by general tradition and above all keeping in mind Desportes, I therefore settled on the 1607 edition, but I am still not quite sure that this was the right decision. At any rate the prospective reader, either of Malherbe or of Desportes, can easily refer to whichever text he wishes. It was just fortunate for me that so few lines were affected by variants, and the issue demonstrates another basic principle of critical editions—there can be no mechanical rules for the selection of the basic text. It is only after prolonged study of the poet and his works that one can attempt to decide intuitively what is right in a particular case.

The question of dating editions is not usually very difficult for sixteenth-century French lyric poetry. Very early in the period are found the beginnings of the *dépôt légal*, the requirement that all books have a royal permit, usually with the censor's certificate. This permit or *privilège* is in the form of an act approved by the king and the parlement giving to a particular individual the exclusive right to publish and sell a certain book for a certain number of years. The author who received such a *privilège* usually turned it over to a *libraire* who then had the exclusive right to print and distribute copies for sale, reproducing in the volume a facsimile of the dated *privilège*.[9]

In the case of Desportes his poetry is protected by five *privilèges* dated 1573, 1583, 1587, 1597, and 1603. Each is for a period of ten years except for the last two which are both for nine years. The exceptional case of the *privilège* for 1587 which was issued before the expiry of the validity of the one given in 1583 was presumably made necessary by the appearance of pirated editions since this particular document alone contains a sentence specifying penalties which will be imposed in the case of fraudulent copying.

There are a number of pirated editions of Desportes, most of them published surreptitiously in places outside Paris like Lyon, Rouen, or Antwerp. They contain no *privilège* and they generally reproduce the text of an earlier authorized edition. The Antwerp edition of 1580, for instance, is based on the Paris edition of 1575 and the text of the Lyon edition of 1595 is identical to that of the edition which appeared in Paris in 1587.

With the authoritative editions marking the decades and the cumulative variants of the intervening editions punctuating these periods at almost annual intervals, it becomes relatively easy to identify spurious copies and to verify publication dates.

It is always a problem, however, to know how to designate editions conveniently in the listings of variants. Following the practice established by Chamard and Laumonier I decided to use the last two digits of the year in which the edition appeared, ignoring of course those editions without any authority. This worked out very well for published works but when it came to manuscripts the solution was not quite so obvious. Much of Desportes's poetry circulated in manuscript before it was published, in some cases with variants which

[9]See Pierre Liotard, *Edition et librairie: Le Rôle de l'éditeur*, 2e année 1ère leçon (1953).

never appeared in print. Some of these manuscripts were presentation albums with exquisite calligraphy. Those in Desportes's own hand are beautifully clear and elegant but some done by copyists are almost illegible. The handwriting of sixteenth-century clerks is notoriously difficult but I was aided by the fact that most of the poems I had to transcribe from such copies were also to be found in one version or another in reasonably clear script or in printed texts.

I personally heartily dislike variant listings in which manuscripts are identified only by a letter arbitrarily assigned by the editor, and since my publisher felt exactly the same way I was able to use abbreviated manuscript references which, for proof-reading at least, made it unnecessary to check the letter as well as the variant. For example, the Rothschild manuscript IV.2.3 was listed as Roths. IV.2.3 and the Arsenal manuscript 3333 as Ms. Ars. 3333. This system may seem a little clumsy but it is certainly safer for the editor and easier for the reader.

The real drudgery of preparing any critical edition is the routine of collating against a basic text a large number of different editions with an unending stream of variants. They must be listed in a way that makes sense, giving half a verse or a whole verse where necessary so that the reader has no trouble fitting the pieces together. Anyone who has been through twenty or thirty editions of the same work knows how easy it is to assume that the listing of a variant which is clear to the editor will also be clear to everyone else. This is frequently not the case and the editor must make doubly sure that his notations are never ambiguous.

In recent years I have studied with interest several schemes designed to facilitate the chore of collating. Everyone has read about translating machines, and when I first heard of the Hinman Collating Machine I had visions of a similar marvelous mechanical monster which would, however, scan each new edition fed into it, spewing forth variants which the editor had only to line up below the basic text. Alas, neither machine apparently is yet able to replace the human agent. The Hinman Collating Machine is restricted to cases where pagination is identical and where the editor wishes to search for minor textual changes or even such fine detail as evidence of damage to type face which would indicate for example which of two identical editions was printed first.[10] Lining up two volumes in the machine by means of the elaborate system of movable tables, weighted glass plates, and adjustable lenses and lights is rather like getting dishes ready for an electric dish-washer; it makes you wonder if it wouldn't be quicker to do it the old way. The machine is extremely useful where a lot of material has to be processed, but the term "collating" is something of a misnomer since it must be understood in this very special sense.

Another method which has been used with great success for proof-reading at the University of Toronto Press and which could certainly be adapted to collating is to record on tape the text of the basic edition which would then be played for comparison with another version. One practical difficulty would be the number of tapes that would be required for a volume running to two or three hundred pages and, in addition, the question of spelling and punctuation would call for special treatment.

This same problem would present enormous difficulties in the use of the computer where the text of the basic edition and each edition to be compared with it would have to be transferred from IBM cards to tape.[11] Forgetting for the moment that punched cards must be proofread and that the volume of material involved might easily run to 30 editions, each consisting of some 400 sonnets and 200 longer poems, let

[10]Cf. Fredson Bowers, "Some Principles for Scholarly Editions of Nineteenth Century American Authors," *Studies in Bibliography*, XVII (1964), 223–8.

[11]Cf. S. M. Parrish, "Problems in the Making of Computer Concordances," *Studies in Bibliography*, XV (1962), 1–14.

us remember that sixteenth-century poetry is quite inconsistent as far as spelling and punctuation are concerned. Not only do these incidentals differ from one edition to another but they may vary within an edition or even within a poem. I could, for example, quote instances where both Desportes and Malherbe spell the same word in two different ways on the same page. Since the computer will note all such differences, the volume of variants would be as difficult to handle as a comparison of the original texts and there is the additional double possibility of error in transcription.

I do not want to seem pessimistic but I am personally convinced that collating must be done painstakingly by the editor himself. Instead of preparing a typescript of the basic text he may nowadays have it xeroxed but the notation of variants can only be done by using good judgment as to what should be put down and how.

There is still general agreement that the basic text should reproduce the original with the commonly accepted editorial modifications such as differentiation of *i* and *j*, *u* and *v*, along with the elimination of abbreviations and the addition of diacritical marks such as the apostrophe and the grave accents which distinguish between *a* and *à*, *ou* and *où* and so forth, but there are some editors, influenced by the practice of reproducing mediaeval texts diplomatically, who would like to be as uncompromising in their treatment of sixteenth-century editions. This problem is infinitely complicated by the very inconsistencies we have just spoken about and for this reason I still believe that the best practice is to provide in the basic text a faithful copy of the original with only those editorial modifications which are necessary for clarity. No purely orthographic variants need be noted but in the case of substantive ones, I would always follow the orthography of the text concerned. Despite what was said earlier about the special interest variants may have, no function is served by encumbering the text with a welter of trivia.

In reproducing the 1607 edition of Desportes these were the principles which were followed. In the case of the Malherbe commentary the situation was somewhat different. The original is full of abbreviations and it has almost no capitals or punctuation. Here I decided to maintain the original spelling but to write out the abbreviations. I also capitalized and punctuated according to modern usage since the commentary would otherwise have looked something like Molly Bloom's soliloquy in *Ulysses* without perhaps the same reader-interest. I think that one is justified in taking such liberties with prose, particularly where it is not written in a form intended for publication.

After the establishment of the basic text and the variants which accompany it, the editor's remaining task is to provide the reader with suitable notes, glossaries, and indexes. Imbued with his subject he may assume that few explanations are necessary but he is much more likely to feel that every little point of literary, historical, or linguistic interest requires a footnote. It is here that he must exercise that most important of all editorial choices—where not to add a footnote.

I remember that in the first volume of the Desportes, which included mainly occasional verse, epitaphs, *masquarades* and the like, I was very reluctant to abandon quite elaborate historical notes which I had put together to explain the circumstances of composition of these poems. My publisher was adamant, however, and in subsequent volumes I was very grateful that I had been persuaded not to submerge the text in a mass of unnecessary documentation.

In this connection, there are, in general, two main sources of abuse of sixteenth-century poetry, apart from historical allusions. These are classical mythology and petrarchan conceits. The pursuit of either can lead very far afield, the first through Ovid and Catullus to Homer and the second through Sasso, Costanzo, or Tebaldeo to Petrarch himself and even the *troubadours*. We are all only too familiar with the erudite type of footnote which purports to trace such references back to their ultimate source or to give gratuitious analogues which add nothing to the elucidation of the text. The important question concerning every single footnote of any kind is: Is it really necessary?

There are many practical problems connected with setting up, on one page, the basic text with variants and footnotes. The early volumes of my edition of Desportes were criticized by some reviewers because I found it expedient to group together Malherbe's commentary and my own explanatory notes. The fact is that the printer could not adjust pages so as to bring together, without any overlap, four separate variables. Three we could manage and since the Malherbe commentary refers to specific parts of the text, it was decided to incorporate it in the footnotes with Malherbe's name in brackets after each comment. There is no possibility of confusion, only a little annoyance perhaps in having to sort out the two.

No edition of lyric poetry is complete without the necessary table of contents, index of first lines, and index of proper names. A glossary is less essential perhaps, particularly as the Huguet *Dictionnaire de la langue française au XVIᵉ siècle* nears completion, but all of these aids can be prepared only with patient care and an enlightened view of what will be useful or indeed indispensable to the discriminating reader.

There are many ways of looking at the editor's rôle in all of this. From some points of view he might be regarded as a slave dominated by the authority of his poet and the rules laid down by tradition and his particular publisher. In this context he would appear to be constantly seeking an elusive ideal within a framework imposed on him by circumstances which he did not create. There is no doubt about the ideology of the critical edition but, from another point of view, the editor is more like the guiding force behind the scenes, choosing, organizing, and imposing his will on the diverse elements involved.

This is why it seems more appropriate to think of him as a kind of *régisseur* or *entremetteur*. He must start with a creation or the personality of another, it is true, but it is his responsibility to present this concept to the public in a guise which is both authentic and attractive. If his task is well done, no one is aware of his intervention and this is as it should be. Reader and author are brought together in a setting which is mutually satisfying.

This function is eloquently described by Rudler for whom mechanical procedures of any kind were unthinkable. Speaking of the subtle variety of methods one must employ in particular circumstances he summed it all up when he wrote:

En réalité, elles admettent ou exigent, dans la position comme dans la solution des problèmes, autant de liberté que de discipline, d'imagination que de tact, de décision que de prudence, de force que de mesure; l'automatisme n'est jamais absolu dans les œuvres de l'esprit.[12]

BIBLIOGRAPHY

General

Bald, R. C. "Editorial Problems: A Preliminary Survey," *Studies in Bibliography*, III (1950–51), 3–17.

Bowers, Fredson "Some Principles for Scholarly Editions of Nineteenth Century American Authors," *Studies in Bibliography*, XVII (1964), 223–8.

Greg, W. W. "The Rationale of Copy-Text," *Studies in Bibliography*, II (1950–51), 19–36.

Meyer, Bruno "Zur Edition Historische Texte," *Schweizerische Zeitschrift für Geschichte*, I (1951), 177–202.

Morize, André *Problems and Methods of Literary History with Special Reference to Modern French Literature, A Guide for Graduate Students* (Boston: Ginn and Co., 1922).

Rudler, Gustave *Les Techniques de la critique et de l'histoire littéraires en littérature française moderne* (Oxford: The University Press, 1923).

[12]*Op. cit.*, xiv.

Specialized

Balić, P. Carlo "La Tecnica delle Edizioni critiche," *Il Libro et la Biblioteche: Atti del primo congresso bibliologico Francescano internazionale* (Rome, 1950), 189–219. [Deals specifically with Duns Scotus and classical methods.]

Havet, E. *Règles et recommandations générales pour l'établissement des éditions Guillaume Budé* (Paris, 1921). [Deals mainly with classical texts.]

Malone Society, "Rules for the Guidance of Editors of the Society's Reprints," *Collections*, vol. I, part 2 (London: Malone Society Publications).

ENGLISH
TRANSLATORS
OF ERASMUS
1522 – 1557

E. J. Devereux

HE WRITINGS of Desiderius Erasmus had, it is certain, a very great effect on the thought of the English humanists and re-formers of the first half of the sixteenth century, and through them on English thought in general. Erasmus, however, wrote only in Latin, and to spread his ideas and attitudes into the ordinary homes in which renaissance and reformation were to be achieved English translations were needed; and were provided by humanists, reformers, printers, and even by the government. From an account of the translations of Erasmus, then, it is possible to get some concept not only of the influence and reputation he had among the learned, but also of the Erasmian ideas that became current among common readers.[1]

I do not know what he thought of English translation of his books, but he probably approved. He had helped the reformers

[1]The bibliography of English translations of Erasmus on which this paper is based is being prepared for publication by the Oxford Bibliographical Society, and is printed here by kind permission of the Council of the Society.

in their demand for vernacular Bibles when he wrote, in the *Paraclesis* of 1516, of a time to come when the ploughman and the weaver might recite verses of Scripture at their work.[2] The first English translation of one of his works to be published was by Sir Thomas More's daughter Margaret, and almost certainly was not made without his knowledge. There can be no doubt that he would have preferred to see his ideas spread through the vernacular rather than not at all.[3] But whether he would have liked the attitudes of many of his English translators is another matter entirely, for it was in the troubled last years of his life that they were hardest at work, turning him into a supporter of the Royal Supremacy and the English Reformation that had cost the life of his friend More. He accepted a gift from Thomas Cromwell,[4] the patron of many of the translators, and he wrote pious works for Anne Boleyn's father,[5] but left us no judgment of them. In the 1530's some thirty translations of his books were made in England; another ten followed in the 1540's; and axes were ground in many of them, one way or another.

The tone was set by the first translation known to have been made. In 1522 William Tyndale was a tutor in the house of Sir John Walsh at Little Sodbury, where he taught and studied and prepared himself for his life's work of translating the Scriptures. At table he argued with "great-beneficed" visitors, a habit that naturally led to trouble with Lady Walsh, who suggested that his views in theology could not be as good as those of the great and the wealthy. Tyndale answered with an appeal from his own obscurity to the fame of Erasmus; he finished a translation of the *Enchiridion Militis Christiani*,

[2]*Opera Omnia*, ed J. Clericus (10 vols., Leyden, 1703–1706), cited as *Opera*; v, 140.

[3]*Opus Epistolarum Erasmi*, ed. P. S. Allen, H. M. Allen, and H. W. Garrod (12 vols., Oxford, 1906–1958), cited as Allen; viii, 176, where certain books are said to be suitable for translation into the vernacular.

[4]Allen, xi, 233, 296.

[5]Allen, viii, 349; x, 233, 237.

including, we may be sure, the reforming epistle to Paul
Volzius that had been added to the book in 1518, and, as
John Foxe records with obvious satisfaction

after they had read and well perused the same, the doctorly pre-
lates were no more so often called to the house, neither had they
the cheer and countenance when they came, as before they had;
which thing they marking, and well perceiving, and supposing
no less but it came by the means of Master Tyndale, refrained
themselves, and at last utterly withdrew, and came no more
there.[6]

What happened to it is open to speculation. A copy passed
to Tyndale's merchant patron Humphrey Monmouth, who
had copies made by his scrivener,[7] one of which was probably
used by the reforming printer John Byddell for the first printed
edition in November 1533. Byddell's text, however, could have
been the translation made by Thomas Artour, who had died
in the previous year.[8] At least ten reprints followed in the
sixteenth century to bring Erasmus's *philosophia Christi* and
the conceit of the weapon of the Christian knight to the
English common reader. So it seems likely that the first translation of Erasmus was the most popular of all, and no doubt
the most influential as well.

The first printed English translation of Erasmus was a
family concern, Margaret Roper's *Precatio Dominica*, which
was printed with a preface by the More family tutor Richard
Hyrde in 1524. There is no known copy of the first edition,
which was probably printed by Wynkyn de Worde,[9] but
Hyrde's preface clearly implies that the text had been printed

[6]John Foxe, *Acts and Monuments,* ed. Josiah Pratt (London, 1877),
v, 116.

[7]*Letters and Papers, Foreign and Domestic, of the Reign of Henry VIII,*
ed. J. S. Brewer, J. Gairdner, and R. H. Brodie (21 vols., London,
1862–1932), cited as *L&P*; iv, document 4282.

[8]John Bale, *Index Britanniae Scriptorum,* ed. R. L. Poole with the help
of Mary Bateson (Oxford, 1902), 429.

[9]*Typographical Antiquities,* begun by Joseph Ames and augmented by
William Herbert, ed. T. F. Dibdin (4 vols., London, 1810–1819), no. 329.

under his supervision by October 1, 1524. The book was a
humanist experiment, the result of study, by double-translation from Latin to English to Latin, in the More household
school;[10] this is shown by the inclusion of the long preface
addressed to Frances S[taverton], which must be one of the
first serious discussions of the education of women. Perhaps
its appearance in print was meant as a special reward for
the efforts of the "yong, vertuous and well lerned gentyl-
woman of .xix. yere of age," as the titles of the extant editions
call her. Erasmus certainly knew of her studies; for in the
same year he dedicated a book to her,[11] and had Magdalia in
the colloquy *Abbatis et Eruditae* cite the "Moricae" of England as examples of learned women;[12] he did not, however,
mention her translation.

The following year saw the first business venture in English
translation of Erasmus when Thomas Berthelet produced a
reprint of the *Precatio Dominica*, his own version of the
Dicta Sapientum and *Mimi Publiani* from Erasmus's *Opuscula Aliquot*, and the French humanist Gentian Hervet's
De Immensa Dei Misericordia. Fortunately, for us if not for
him, he neglected to exhibit his copy to the authorities and
was called to answer for unruly printing, a hard reward for
the publication of three orthodox works and a sermon by
Bishop John Fisher.[13] The connection with More, Fisher, and
Margaret Pole, the Countess of Salisbury, Hervet's patroness,
doubtless helped him out of any trouble; and his testimony
both dates the printing of the books between October 12,
1524 and March 12, 1525–26 and identifies himself and
Margaret Roper as the translators of the two anonymous books.

[10]See J. A. Gee, "Margaret Roper's English Version of Erasmus' *Precatio
Dominica* and the Apprenticeship Behind Early Tudor Translation,"
Review of English Studies, xii (1937), 257–71.
[11]Allen, v, 366–7.
[12]*Opera*, i, 746.
[13]A. W. Reed, "The Regulation of the Book Trade Before the Proclamation of 1538," *Transactions of the Bibliographical Society*, xv (1917–1919),
166–9.

Of the three the most interesting is Hervet's which contains an enthusiastic preface that shows how highly Erasmus was esteemed by the young humanists and contains the first clear statement on why Erasmus should be translated. Hervet thought, as he told the Countess, that

it shuld be a good dede, if for your ladysships pleasure it were printed & spred abrode: and where as afore lerned men only dyd get out both pleasure and great frute in redyng of this boke, now euery man as wel rude as lerned maye haue this sermon of the mercy of god as common vnto hym as the mercy of god it selfe is.

Its author could be no more flattered by Hervet "than the son with a candell may be made clerer"; truth had been hidden and the search for truth forbidden when Erasmus was a young man, but he had "digged vp many lymmes of trouth, or at the lest he hath restored vs free liberte to serche her."

Whan from this man there can come out nothyng but both it is excedyng profitable and of euery syde all perfect, me thynketh that this litell treatise beying in euery poynt as perfect as any other be in profit, nat only gyueth no place but also greatly passeth: for where afore all the workes that he made were profitable but specially to one kynde of men, his Prouerbes, his Newe Testament, and many other treatises only to lerned men, of the boke of the Instruction of princis the most profit redoundeth to princis. This boke only with the boke called the knyfe or wepon of a Christen sowdiour hath so far spredde abrode his frutefull branches that there is no man but great frute gather he may out of it. . . .

Hervet was to belong to the Counter-Reformation. Already it can be seen that there was a Protestant Erasmus for Tyndale and a Catholic one for the More and Pole families.

On June 20, 1529 the first openly polemic translation was printed at Antwerp by Johannes Hoochstraten, or "Hans Luft" of "Marburg," to use the false imprint in which the reformers combined the name of Luther's printer and the Protestant university to make their books even more offensive

to the unreformed. It was the *Paraclesis*, the work in which
Erasmus had argued the case for vernacular Bibles. The
translator was one of Tyndale's associates, following his
leader's suggestion that it was a book containing reasons that
opponents of the English Bible could not answer.[14] He was
no doubt also striking at More, who, though well known as
Erasmus' friend, was the official spokesman against Tyndale.
It was a good hit, and it was also the only translation of Erasmus to come directly from the Antwerp exiles; perhaps they
agreed with Tyndale's second thoughts on Erasmus as one
whose tongue made elephants of gnats for the sake of an
exihibition.[15]

Through the next couple of years Berthelet continued to
print English translations of Erasmus, reprints of his earlier
publications, and new translations of the *Declamatio De Morte*
and *De Contemptu Mundi*, orthodox pious books that were
neither exciting to the reformers nor obnoxious to the authorities, bearing testimony of little besides the printer's fidelity to
Erasmian thought.

In 1532 the reformers took up Erasmus again, this time
not to needle More but to spread throughout England the
ideas that would help so greatly to form and to bring about
the *via media* of the English Church. The first man to see
the value Erasmus had was Richard Taverner, one of the
young Cantabrigians who had brought heresy into Cardinal
Wolsey's new college at Oxford in 1529. He offered his
services to Cromwell, who procured him a pension. Not long
afterwards he dedicated to Cromwell a translation of Erasmus'
Encomium Matrimonii, with a preface to show how it opposed

[14]In *The Obedience of a Christian Man* in 1528: William Tyndale,
Doctrinal Treatises, ed. Henry Walter (Cambridge, 1848), 161–62.
The "Hans Luft" books are described in W. Nijhoff and M. E. Kronen-
berg, *Nederlandsche Bibliographie van 1500–1540* (The Hague, 1923–
1961).
[15]*Ibid.*, p. 357. The phrase appears in Erasmus' *Adagia* as "Elephantum
ex musca fecis." *Chil.* I, *Cent.* I, *Ad.* LXIX.

"bachelershyp, a forme of lyuynge bothe barren and vn-naturall." This was not really fair, as Erasmus had written it as a rhetorical exercise for Lord Mountjoy in 1498, though he prided himself in a light moment on its success, as shown by Mountjoy's outliving three wives and planning to take a fourth.[16] Taverner's dedication to Cromwell, however, tells how he

> began besily to reuolue in mynd, how he, agayne on hys parte myght somwhat declare his feruent zele of herte towards you. Which he thus reuoluynge, loo sodenly (as god wolde) a certayne Epystle of Doctour Erasmus, deuysed in commendacion of wed-locke, offered it selfe vnto his syght. Which so sone as he began to reade, he thought it a thynge full necessarye and expedyent, to translate it in to our vulgere tong, & so vnder your noble pro-tection to communicate it to the people, namely when he con-sidered the blynd superstition of men and women, which cease nat day by day to professe & vowe perpetuall chastyte before or they suffyciently knowe themselues & thinfirmitie of theyr nature.

The implications seem clear: popularizing the concept of things indifferent to salvation could weaken the established power of the Church and English translations from Erasmus and other thinkers could spread such ideas if protection of writers and printers could be had. There is little doubt that, as Dr. J. K. McConica has pointed out, the book sealed the bargain between Cromwell and Taverner.[17]

Word seems to have got around that Cromwell's patron-age would be given for English versions of Erasmus' works, particularly those straightforward enough for plain people, those that contained the simple Erasmian *philosophia Christi* in implied contrast to the formal theological argument of the conservative side, and those that somehow supported the idea

[16]Allen, i, 18.

[17]Dr. McConica discussed Taverner and Cromwell in his Oxford thesis "The Continuity of Humanist Ideas During the English Reformation to 1558," the basis for his book, *English Humanists and Reformation Politics* (Oxford, 1965). Taverner's letters are in *L&P*, v, documents 1762 and 1763.

of Royal Supremacy in the Church. On July 2, 1533 a young Fellow of King's College, Cambridge, Martin Tyndall, sent Cromwell his version of the Epistle to Jodocus Jonas, in which Erasmus had written short lives of the two great early reformers, John Colet and John Vitrier.[18] His letter shows a certain amount of organization; he assumed that Cromwell himself would approve the work or reject it, that it should be checked by Taverner, and that it might have been well to have shown it first to William Marshall. His translation is lost, but we have his word that it did not flatter the "peevish Popish." On November 15 the first edition of the *Enchiridion Militis Christiani* appeared, printed by Wynkyn de Worde for John Byddell, who not long before had been de Worde's "servant," but who from 1533 was prominent in the publication of reforming books, particularly translations of Erasmus, in which he may have been supported by Cromwell.[19] While it was respectably orthodox in its teaching, the book had, in the Epistle to Volzius, an open appeal for the reformation of the Church and a statement that a worldly Church need not be obeyed against a higher authority. For the armour of the Christian knight, Byddell wrote in a verse preface, "Erasmus is the onely furbyssher."

The translation of Erasmus that passed through Cromwell's hands in 1533 are not open and vehement attacks, but merely works arguing the need for reform. It was towards the end of the year that Henry VIII told the French Ambassador that he had been holding back the printers, but would now turn them loose against the Pope,[20] and, as Chapuys reported from time to time to Charles V, there followed an almost immediate flow of English books of theology watered down for the common reader, polemic, and simple vituperation.[21]

---

[18]*L&P*, vi, documents 751 and 752.

[19]Cromwell paid accounts to or for Byddell at about this time. *L&P*, vi, document 299, ii and vii, document 923, iv.

[20]*L&P*, vi, document 1501.

[21]Chapuys' reports are summarized in *L&P*.

In April 1534 Cromwell, acting on an earlier promise, helped finance publication of a translation of the *Symbolum sive Catechismus*, a book that Erasmus had written for Thomas Boleyn.[22] A more immediately relevant work followed on May 13 when the humanist Thomas Cox sent his translation of the *Paraphrasis* on Titus, showing "how moche and howe straytly we be bounde to obey next God our kyng & souerayne lorde," to the bookseller John Toy, asking him to send it to Cromwell to see whether it would be printed or not.[23] Cox's preface gave thanks for the Royal Supremacy that had delivered England from the "rauenyng mouth" of the Pope and the "thraldome of yll bysshops." Evidently Cromwell approved, and the book was soon printed by Byddell. And in September the colloquy *Pietas Puerilis* was translated and submitted by Henry Dowes, Gregory Cromwell's tutor, as yet another work of simple piety, a particularly clear exposition of the idea of *adiaphora* or things indifferent.[24] The anonymous translation of the *De Esu Carnium*, another adiaphorist book, probably also appeared in 1534.

By the end of the year the campaign of publication was in full swing. On January 5, 1534–35 Byddell brought out a translation of the colloquy *Funus*, satirizing the greedy clergy; he added one of *Exsequiae Seraphicae*, against the regular clergy; and followed through with the dialogue Erasmus denied so often having written, *Julius Exclusus E Coelis*.[25] The character of Pope Julius II caused the nameless translator "often to meruayle at them that say, the Pope of Rome (as they call hym) can not erre"; and no doubt raised the same wonder in readers delighted by the brilliant satire of the dialogue between the Pope and St. Peter.

The conservative side took up arms in the Pilgrimage of

[22]*L&P*, vii, documents 422 and 423.
[23]*L&P*, vii, document 659.
[24]*L&P*, vii, document 1135.
[25]For a full discussion of Erasmus's authorship see W. K. Ferguson, *Erasmi Opuscula* (The Hague, 1933), 38–64.

Grace just as Cromwell was moving to take over the monasteries and suppress shrines in the King's name. An anonymous translator took the colloquy *Peregrinatio Religionis Ergo*, which included an account of a trip by Erasmus and Colet to Canterbury, to argue the government's case. In the colloquy, the translator noted:

Desiderius Erasmus hath set forthe to the quycke ymage, before mennys eyes, the supersticyouse worshype and false honor gyuyn to bones, heddes, iawes, armes, stockes, stones, shyrtes, smokes, cotes, cappes, hattes, shoes, mytres, slyppers, sadles, synges, bedes, gyrdes, bolles, belles, bokes, gloues, ropes, taperes, candelles, bootes, sporres (my breath was almost past me) with many other soche dampnable allusyones of the deuylle to vse theme as goddes contrary to the immaculate scripture of god.

The unreformed, fearing that their days were numbered, "rebelle and make insurrectyones contrary to the ordynaunce of gode, agaynst theyr kynge and liege lorde," in an effort to forestall the King's judgment on their "Sodomiticall actes."

The crushing of the Pilgrims, the abolition of the shrines, the dissolution of the monasteries, and the licensing of Matthew's Bible all raised the hopes of the reformers, who saw the beginnings of a true reformation. In 1537 John Wayland printed a translation of *De Puritate Ecclesiae Christianae*, a commentary on the psalm *Domine Quis Habitabit* that was Erasmus' last work, a characteristic discussion of the need for personal reform. Full of hope, the translator wrote that Erasmus' style was most "swete and melodyous" in the treatise, which

oughte and shall delyte the so moche the more, that he doth shewe this his musyke to accorde with the moost pure expositers of scripture, whome god hath gracyouslye nowe in our tyme raysed vp to the expulsyon of fylthye and grosse errours. . . .

But, even as he wrote, the conscience of the King was concerned about the reformation. The Articles of 1536 (*S.T.C.* 10033) began the conservative reaction; in conjunction with them Marshall had Byddell print a translation of *Exomologesis*, Erasmus's consideration of auricular Confession. In 1538 the Epistle to Balthasar Mercklin was translated to argue the case for the Eucharistic Presence; and no doubt also to support the burning of John Lambert who, for denying it, had been condemned to the stake by the King himself, who appeared at the trial dressed completely in papal white.[26] The conservative tone of the translation is clear at once; the book, the writer noted, treated "the veryte of the body and bloude of oure sauyoure christe in the blyssed sacrament of the alter" and the "dewe vse of the holy masse."

By the end of the decade Erasmus had served his turn as reformer, and translation of his theological or satirical works for the advancement of the English Reformation stopped, as the King moved to end the freedom of religious discussion that had been necessary during his dispute with the Papacy. The Proclamation of 1538 for licensing books, the Act of Six Articles in 1539, and the Act for the Advancement of True Religion in 1543 combined to restore Erasmus to the grammar school;[27] in 1540 Cromwell himself was attainted for having, among other things, had false books of religion spread into all shires, for having had them translated "into our maternal and English tongue," and for affirming the heresies contained in them.[28] He went to execution reciting Erasmus's prayer *In Gravi Morbo*.[29] This put a temporary halt to the career of Erasmus, the apologist of Henry VIII, until 1545 when a translation of *De Sarcienda Ecclesiae Concordia* was published to support the King's charitable exhortation to Parliament not to be too set in their old *mumpsimus* or their

[26]See H. Maynard Smith, *Henry VIII and the Reformation* (London, 1962), 446–50.

[27]Respectively, S.T.C. 7790, and Statutes of the Realm 31 Henry VIII, c. 14 and 34 & 35 Henry VIII, c. 1.

[28]L&P, xv, document 498.

[29]C. S. Coldwell, *The Prayers of Erasmus* (London, 1872), vii, cited by Helen C. White in *The Tudor Books of Private Devotion* (Madison, 1951), 162. An English text of the prayer is in Foxe, v, 403.

new *sumpsimus*. The translator, perhaps naturally enough, was Taverner.[30]

Not all of the English translations that appeared in the 1530's were meant to serve the purposes of reformation. Berthelet kept on publishing humanist works, perhaps feeling that he got enough polemic in books such as Richard Morison's *Apomaxis* that he had to produce as King's Printer;[31] and he added translations of the pacifist adage *Dulce Bellum Inexpertis* in 1534, *Virginis Et Martyris Comparatio* by Thomas Paynell in 1537, and *De Praeparatione Ad Mortem* in 1538. Wynkyn de Worde's publication of Robert Whittington's *De Civilitate Morum Puerilium* in 1532 was merely to add another text to that grammarian's formidable list. Robert Redman's publication of translations of the *Concio De Puero Jesu* and *De Laude Artis Medicae* had little to do with Cromwell's reformers; and the sermon from the *Liturgia Virginis Lauretanae*, printed by Robert Wyer in 1533 or 1534, again seems a simple work of piety, although its exhortation to proper devotion may well have had some place in the reformers' plans.

From 1539 Erasmus was seen as a scholar rather than a reformer. Taverner brought out no fewer than six booklets of Erasmian proverbs, and the Bible printer Richard Grafton and Nicholas Udall joined in a translation of two books of the *Apophthegmata*. Only John Gough, who had been constantly in trouble as a publisher of Protestant books since as early as 1528,[32] kept up with the adage *Sileni Alcibiadis*, translated to show how far the "Spirituallte" were "from *the* perfite trade and lyfe of Christe"; nobody else would take the risk with Cromwell gone.

In 1545 Erasmus' works found a new patron in Catherine Parr. In the spring Myles Coverdale's English abstract of the *Enchiridion* was printed at Antwerp, under the false imprint

[30]Anthony Wood, *Athenae Oxonienses* (London, 1691), i, 145. The King's speech is reprinted by H. Maynard Smith, 211–12.
[31]See *L&P*, xi, document 1481 from Morison to Cromwell; "Mr. Berthelet stays the printing of my book; he will know your pleasure."
[32]E. G. Duff, *A Century of the English Book Trade* (London, 1905), 58.

of "Adam Anonimus"; but in July Grafton published Philip
Gerrard's translation of the moral colloquy *Epicureus*, dedicated to the Prince of Wales and carrying the imprint of
the "Printer too the Princes Grace." Erasmus obviously was
about to be drawn into the next stage of the English Reformation.

By late September the Queen was asking the Princess Mary
to have her English translation of the *Paraphrasis* on the
Gospel of St. John corrected by her chaplain Francis Malet
and sent to her; and urging her further to allow it to be
published under her name.[33] At about the same time she
received a translation of Luke by Udall, with a preface pro-
claiming himself "by many degrees inferior to the others
whom I heare *that* your highnesse hath appoincted to the
translating of the other partes." Thomas Key soon submitted
his version of Mark, with a letter praising the Queen for
having "commaunded certayne well learned persons to translate the said worke." Two unknown scholars took care of
Matthew and Acts. The manuscripts were given to Udall for
preparation for the press; and all was ready for the right
moment, which was to be as soon as possible after the death
of Henry VIII.

The new King, the "young Josiah," as the reformers called
him, succeeded at the beginning of 1547; and by the end
of the summer there appeared the new *Injunctions* (S.T.C.
10088–93), the seventh of which ordered all parish churches
to buy the Great Bible and

the Paraphrasis of Erasmus also in Englishe vpon the Gospelles,
& thesame sette vp in some conuenient place, within the sayed
Churche, that they haue cure of, wheras their Parishioners maye
moste commodiously resorte vnto thesame, and reade the same.

The twelfth added that ministers under the degree of B.D.
should buy Latin and English New Testaments and the
Paraphrases, "and diligently study thesame, conferring the

[33]MS. Cotton Vespasian F III. 37.

one with the other." Through the year Grafton's associate, Edward Whitchurch, who shared his service book patent,[34] worked steadily through the large volume, and at the end of January 1548, just six months after the *Injunctions* were published, the Queen's work appeared in print, with a dedication to the King by Udall and dedications of each section to Catherine Parr. As Udall wrote to the King,

. . . when I dooe in my mynde make a comparison of you three together, Erasmus in wryting this Paraphrase, Quene katerine dowagier in procuryng thesame to bee turned into Englishe, and your highnesse in publishyng thesame by your godly iniunccions . . . me semeth I dooe well note Erasmus to haue dooen the leste acte of the three.

A second volume followed, without either Catherine Parr or Udall to help the printer, who sought the patronage of the Duchess of Somerset; Whitchurch got Coverdale to act as general editor, and Coverdale seems to have translated Romans, Corinthians, and Galatians as his share, leaving the rest to John Old, a friend of the printer, who did everything but Titus, for which he sought out Leonard Cox and asked him to revise his old version.

England was indifferent. Stephen Gardiner had to be removed from the Council for his violent objections to the book that Erasmus had written "aboue 26 yeres a goo, when his penne was wanton," and the translation, of which he agreed with Somerset that a slumber might be pardonable in a long work, but argued that "this translator was a sleppe when he began."[35] But nobody else seems to have worried about anything but the ten or twelve shillings the book cost, and Catherine Parr's dream of an Erasmian England came to nothing. It is depressing to see it end in the hypocrisy of the monopolist Christopher Barker, who gave up the patent

[34]*Calendar of Patent Rolls, 1 Edward VI,* (London, 1924), i, 190. Grafton had succeeded Berthelet as King's Printer on April 22, 1547; *ibid.,* 187.

[35]J. A. Muller, *The Letters of Stephen Gardiner* (Cambridge, 1933), letters 130, 131, 133, 135, and 136.

for printing the *Paraphrases* in 1583 for the relief of the poor of the Stationers' Company.[36]

The other Edwardian translators of Erasmus show only a concern for the ever-growing addiction of Englishmen to theological argument and disputes on the precise meanings of crucial words. Each is defensive about his translation, prepared for an onslaught of questions about his choice of words, and more or less satirical about the freedom of discussion the Protectorate allowed.

In 1549 Berthelet printed his last new Erasmus text, Thomas Chaloner's version of *Moriae Encomium*. Whether we should see in this Berthelet's comment on the undoing of the *via media* and on the way he himself had been dumped to allow Grafton to become King's Printer I cannot say, but one is tempted to speculate. The translation is at least partly directed against the contentious age and the new reformers who "condemne all thinges, that fully square not with theyr owne rules." Chaloner felt the need to explain each divergence from the Latin text, any one of which might "be thought by some cunnyng translatours a deadly sinne," and to guide his readers in the interpretation of the satire.

The Northampton divorce question was also much in public discussion when a friend of Nicholas Lesse learned from a group of men "of most sound iudgement" that Erasmus had written wisely and well on divorce in his *Annotationes In Novum Testamentum*. Concerned about the fact that disputes on divorce were "nowe in al mens mouths," he urged Lesse on to the translation of the relevant section, in the hope that Erasmian calmness might help settle the question.

The most interesting Edwardian translation is Edmund Becke's *Two dyaloges wrytten in laten by the famous clerk D. Erasmus of Roterdam*, printed at Canterbury by John Mychell about 1551. Becke's translations of the colloquies *De Rebus Ac Vocabulis* and *Cyclops* were clearly intended as satire on the more radical and vehement reformers, particularly "Polyphemus or the gospeller," Erasmus' ironic picture of his disciple Felix Rex piously defending the truth by raising three lumps on a Franciscan's head with the Erasmus New Testament.[37]

In his preface Becke writes of the "daungerous dayes" in which all readers stood ready to fall upon any translation, "be it that the matter be neuer so base"; and argued that he had observed

the thyng which in translacyon is of all other most necessary and requisite, that is to saye, to rendre the sence & the very meaning of the author, not so relygyouslie addicte to translate worde for worde, but so the sence of the author is oftentimes corrupted & depraued, and neyther the grace of the one tonge nor yet of the other is truely obserued or aptlie expressed. The lerned knoweth *that* euery tonge hathe his peculyer proprietie, phrase, manner of locucion, enargies and vehemencie, which so aptlie in any other tong can not be expressed.

The reign of Edward VI passed away in contant disputation on doctrine and meaning, a form of controversy in which the humane Erasmus had little place. The restoration of the connection with Rome at the accession of Mary in 1553 was marked by the publication by William Riddell of *Two Epistles wherein is declared the brainsicke headines of the Luthererans*, translated by Henry Lord Stafford, as John Strype comments, "to shew his compliance with these times."[38] In the following year the Queen's Printer John Cawood published an anonymous translation of the Epistle to Conradus Pellicanus, another work in which Erasmus reaffirmed his belief in the Real Presence. But there was no new campaign of translation and publication, under Mary or Elizabeth, and Erasmus dropped out of English religious controversy, after a quarter of a century in which his writings, in English translations, had been used by all sides of the Reformation.

[37]C. R. Thompson, *The Colloquies of Erasmus* (Chicago and London, 1965), 415–16.
[38]John Strype, *Ecclesiastical Memorials* (Oxford, 1822), iii, ii, 180.

THREE TUDOR EDITORS
OF THOMAS MORE

Germain Marc'hadour

URING HIS imprisonment in the Tower
of London— April 17, 1534 to July 6, 1535—
More wrote extensively whenever he was not
altogether deprived of paper and ink. Besides
letters and prayers, two books of this period
have come down to us: the English *Dialogue
of Comfort against Tribulation*, and the Latin *Expositio
Passionis*. Not only were these not printed in More's lifetime,
but there was no question of printing them in England while
Henry VIII and Edward VI were on the throne, since they
came from the pen of a "traitor," and several passages in the
Dialogue, thinly disguised by the Turkish occupation in
Hungary, bore all too clearly on the situation brought about
by a temporal prince usurping spiritual power. The same ban
applied to the treatises More had composed in the few
months preceding his arrest, when he was already out of
favour and constantly maligned and hunted by the Crom-
well-Boleyn administration. One is a short treatise on "How
to receive the blessed Body of Our Lord"; another (unfinished) is a *History of the Passion*, but it tackles only the
preliminary stage, and its main development (close to thirty

folio pages) is the institution of the Eucharist. Both, therefore, continue, as it were, More's last printed book: *An
Answer to . . . the "Supper of the Lord,"* which was on sale
by Christmas 1533.

As soon as the Catholic Mary Tudor ascended the throne—
July 19, 1553—the possibility of printing Thomas More again
was eagerly seized upon, and the *Dialogue of Comfort,* a
masterpiece in more than one respect, had obvious priority.
Its editio princeps was finished by Richard Tottell on November 18, 1553, a bare four months after Mary's accession. This
quarto of 330 pages (*S.T.C.* 18082, Gibson's *Preliminary
Bibliography* no. 51, listing eleven extant copies), was, as far
as we know, the first book to come from Tottell's press. The
paper is rather poor, and the typing rather crude. For the
initial Z in Zacheus' name, no capital Z was available: in
the first instance, the letter is left blank, in the second a
capital N turned on its side is substituted, and later a low
case z (M²v, M³). The Latin quotations are often misspelt,
as if written under dictation, with the characteristic English
confusions already noted by Erasmus : ne*ss*imus for ne*sc*imus
(I, 16), *en* for *in*, obedience for obediens (I, 19), and some
words are distorted beyond recognition, for example, L²
where transi*ens* becomes trans*itus*.

William Rastell, More's nephew and sole printer in his
most productive years—from the autumn of 1529 to the end
of 1533—had no hand in Tottell's edition of the *Dialogue,*
which was out several weeks before Rastell returned from
overseas. Had Rastell teleguided the venture, he would no
doubt have insisted upon a minimum of marginal references
and some prefatory material, neither of which appears in
Tottell. When the hour came for a second edition, Rastell
provided the printers with a substantially different manuscript, never even alluding to the 1553 edition.

This is the more surprising as Tottell was one of the three
printers who came together for the production of the folio

English Workes of More (*S.T.C.* 18076), sponsored if not masterminded by Rastell, completed and dedicated by him to the Queen in April 1557. Tottell's partners were John Waley and John Cawood; the latter alone, probably on account of his being royal printer, put his monogram on the title page. There is no evidence that Tottell, in this Morean "miscellany," was put in charge of the portion which he had tackled earlier on his own. The *Dialogue* is placed (pp. 1139–1264) before the two Eucharistic treatises which, as we have said, were written prior to More's imprisonment. Later editors of the *Dialogue of Comfort*, as well as of More's other works, have commonly used the text of this 1557 folio. For one thing, it looks so admirably careful, faithful, and thorough, and besides it is available in many more copies than any other early edition: Ramage, in 1948, listed 25 copies in the British Isles, while Bishop, in 1950, listed 22 copies in the United States, but at least 120 are known to be extant in the world, quite a few in private hands. Although these *Workes* are usually referred to as Rastell's edition, one should not assume that More's nephew and literary executor personally contributed the marginal glosses or established the text. At least for the theological or devotional works, a much more likely annotator is Thomas Paynell, a priest and former monk, who (according to the subtitle of the Table) "collected and gathered together the many matters contained in this book." The nature of the references—scriptural rather than legal or historical—points to a cleric, not a lawyer as Rastell was. As compiler of the table of contents he takes almost all his clues from the marginalia, seldom including items not already singled out in the margins.

In 1573 John Fowler, a recusant from Bristol, printed the *Dialogue of Comfort* at Antwerp in "smaller volume than it was in before" (ijv); it is a neat octavo of 456 pages (*S.T.C.* 18083). Gibson's *Bibliography* (no. 52) locates 21 copies, but others are known to exist, one in my own "Morianum" at

Angers. Fowler claims to have produced a critical edition, with "many places restored and corrected by conference of sundry copies" together. *Sundry* seems to imply more than the two printed editions we have described, although it might mean several exemplars of the same edition, marked by perceptive and well-informed readers, one of whom, perhaps, being John Harris, More's last secretary, and Fowler's father-in-law. His division of chapters at the end of book 2, tallying neither with Tottell's nor with Rastell's, may be evidence of a manuscript model different from those of his predecessors. The new division, however, might be part of the "correction" procedure. If *restored* means brought closer to the original, *corrected* presumably involves some measure of "improvement" on the original. The many glosses added by Fowler to enucleate the allusions to contemporary England evaporate all the artistic flavour of More's Hungarian mystification. On the title page, the biblical verse "Non desis plorantibus in consolatione" (Ecclus. 7:38)—never used by More despite its perfect relevance to his purpose—is prefixed as a text to the 430 pages of his "consolation" sermon. A layman and a *quondam* schoolmaster—which meant a classical scholar—Fowler contributes various references to Roman or Greek authors, for example Cicero's *De Senectute* (2r), Aristotle's *Ethics* (51r) with its Latin rendering: *Virtus versatur circa difficilia.* Maybe some Louvain friend helped him too, for he gives the reference in Aquinas' *Summa* for the virtue of *eutrapelia* in book 2, ch. I. (57r) and, alone of the three Tudor editors, he accentuates this Greek word correctly. Forms like *eien* or *manhead* had grown obsolete by 1557 and even more so by 1573: yet, while he changes *eien* to *eyes*, Fowler keeps *manhead* against *manhood* from the 1557 edition. The grammar of More he tacitly amends, as was already pointed out by Joseph Delcourt in his *Essai sur la langue de Sir Thomas More* (Paris, 1914, p. 367 ff.): the 1553 and 1557 editions, as well as the Oxford and the London manuscripts, have in book I, ch. 19: "Though Abraham had not as he did indeed far excel Lazar in merit," which is correct syntax by early Tudor standards. Fowler tidied this up into: "Though Abraham had not (as he did indeed) far excelled Lazar in merit" (37v).

Nothing, however, is more striking in the procedure of these successive editor-publishers than their handling of biblical quotations in More's posthumous *Dialogue*. Tottell does not locate a single passage. Paynell provides scriptural references whenever he can find them. Fowler lifts these from the 1557 folio, adding a few of his own and occasionally pruning off those he thinks redundant: thus *Johan.* 14 is repeated twice in close succession on p. 1140A of the folio, Fowler has it only once. My attention was attracted to such discrepancies when I began a systematic inventory of scriptural lore in More's writings. Among his favourite verses is Philippians I:23, which he translates: "I long to be dissolved and to be with Christ." Incidentally, he is the only Tudor translator to use *I long*, all the others have *desire*, which was already Wycliffe's rendering. As for the Latin, I found that in all instances where More gives it, it reads: "Cupio dissolvi et esse cum Christo," except in book III, ch. 22, where *cupio* is replaced by *desiderium habens*. This rather cumbrous participle—a close transliteration of the Greek original *epithumian ekhôn*—is the Vulgate reading, yet it never became traditional. At least as early as Tertullian's day it was supplanted by *cupio*, which is handier and probably conveys a stronger sense of craving. The Church herself endorsed this kind of plebiscite against the Vulgate, since she uses *cupio* several times in the second nocturns of the Breviary. It seems that even exegetes, not excepting Jerome, instinctively prefer *cupio* whenever they do not have their finger running on the pagina sacra. The word is not to be found here in Nicolas de Lyre nor in the *Glossa ordinaria*, because these are directly exegetical. Erasmus himself, in his version of the New Testament, uses Anselm's *desiderans*, and in the Annotations he has Augustine's *concupiscentiam habens*; but in his other works, from the 1499 *disputatiuncula* with Colet, to the 1534 *Praeparatio ad Mortem*, he consistently writes *cupio*. So do St John Fisher and Luther, Cochlaeus and Eckius, Beatus Rhenanus and Faber of Vienna, so do the Scholastics and Pico della Mirandola. Alone against this "turba magna" and only once against his own wont, Thomas More seemed to cling to the clumsy Vulgate phrasing in the third book of his dialogue as quoted in the 1557 edition: *desiderium habens dissolui et esse cum Christo, multo magis melius parmanere autem in carne necessarium propter vos* (1250B). The same wording occurs in Fowler except that spelling and punctuation are better: *desiderium habens dissolui & esse cum Christo, multo magis melius: Permanere autem in carne, necessarium propter vos* (192v). Was More then, for once, not trusting his memory, but transcribing the Vulgate with his finger on the line? Yet, only a few months later, *cupio* reappears at least twice in the *Expositio Passionis*, (1689 ed., p. 151, col. 1, line 42 f. 19r of More's autograph; and p. 168, towards the end of col. 2 f. 103v of the autograph), again in the prayer which More wrote in July 1535 after his condemnation (*Workes*, p. 1417 F). Moreover, answering a letter from his daughter late in 1534, that is, much at the same date as his *Dialogue*, More thanked Margaret for quoting St Paul's *Cupio dissolvi* (Rogers, *The Correspondence of Sir Thomas More*, no. 211, p. 544, line 13). The lonely exception remained a puzzle until I was able to check the passage in the unglossed and unedited 1553 text, where it reads: "Cupio dissolui & esse cum Christo bonum autem michi manere propter vos" (T¹v). So no erratic block remains in our path.

This test case led me to collating the three editions from the same biblical angle, and I found that a similar tampering had taken place in scores of cases. I have not consulted the early manuscript copies, but Professor Louis Martz, who is establishing the text of the *Dialogue* for the Yale edition, confirmed my verdict in a letter of October 4, 1965: "Everything that you say is quite in line with my own study of the Corpus Christi manuscript, especially on the subject of the biblical quotations. . . ." The first chapter of the book quotes the Book of Sirach: "Honora medicum propter necessitatem enim ordinauit eum altissimus. Honor thou *the* phisicio*n*, for him hath *the* high god ordened for thi necessitie." (Tottell, A5v) Paynell provides the reference, Ecclus. 38, and retouches More's Latin by changing *enim* to *etenim* as in the Vulgate. The result, on p. 1142H of the folio, is: "Honora medicum propter necessitatem, etenim ordinavit eum altissimus: Honour thou the phisicion, for him hath the hygh God ordeyned for thy necessitie." Whoever—editor or printer— was responsible for the punctuation created an obvious discrepancy between the Latin and the English. Fowler (7r) brings them together: "Honora medicu*m*: propter necessitatem etenim ordinauit eum Altissimus, Honour thou *the* Physicion, for him hath the high God ordened for thy necessitie." It appears that Fowler, with his eye on More's rendering, re-punctuated the Latin to fit the English.

In book 1, ch. 8, Paynell, though he gives the reference Josu. 7, resists the temptation to tamper with More's text, which reads, as in 1553, apart from minute spelling differences: "Fili mi, da gloriam deo Israel, et confitere et indica mihi quid feceris et ne abscondas. Mine own son, give glory to the God of Israel, and confess and shew me what thou hast done, and hide it not." (B5r and 1148G) But Fowler borrows the Vulgate text altogether: "da gloria*m* Domino Deo Israël . . .," and accordingly retouches More's version: "give glorie to *the* Lord God of Israel . . ." (17r).

In book I, ch. 10, Fowler goes further than Paynell again in aligning More's Latin on the Vulgate of Phil. 2:4. Instead of "Quaerentes non quae sua sunt, sed quae aliorum," he has: "No*n* quae sua sunt singuli co*n*siderantes, sed ea quae aliorum." And yet, this time, he respects More's rendering: "Seke not for your owne profite, but for other folks" (22v), which jars with the Latin in Fowler, while agreeing with that in the other two.

The gross oversight in Tottell's "They shall come . . . with their hands full of corn in their hands" (ch. 13, C5v) was easily amended by his two successors into "their handfuls of corn" (1154 H and 28 f). The text is from Psalm. 125:7. Of greater interest, also in this chapter, is Luke 24:26, which More quotes again in book 3, ch. 26. In Tottell, it reads here, "An nesciebatis quia oportebat Christum pati, et sic introire in regnum suum? Know you not that Christ must suffer and so go into his kindom?" (C6r) and in the third book it reads: "Nesciebatis quia oportebat Christum pati et sic introire in regnum suum? Knew yet not that Christ must suffer passion, and by that way enter into his kingdom?" (U7v). The Latin text is unchanged apart from the omission of a comma and of "an." The rendering is more explicit, more emphatic in the second instance, where More is inculcating the necessity for the Christian to follow the same painful path as Christ. To account for More's Latin, it may be useful to put side by side Luke 24:26, "Nonne haec oportuit pati Christum, et ita intrare in gloriam suam" as correctly quoted in the letter against Frith (*Workes* 838C; Rogers, *op. cit.* no. 190, p. 451, line 393) and Luke 24:46: "Sic oportebat Christum pati et resurgere." In the *Dialogue* citation, More substitutes the phrase *oportebat Christum pati*, from Luke 24:46, for the *oportuit pati Christum* of Luke 24:26—an unconscious liberty which he could not afford in his confutation of Frith, when controversy made it imperative to quote with perfect accuracy. To come back to the *Dialogue*, Paynell and Fowler give the reference as Luke 24 in the first book, yet leave the text substantially untouched. But in the third book, they both make it conform to the Vulgate and yet leave the English as

it was. "Nesciebatis" has gone, yet its counterpart "Knewe
you not" (p. 1260 D) or "know ye not" (210v) has been
retained, which may give a distorted view of More as a
translator. It is also noteworthy that both, in the second
instance, give the reference as "Luc. vlt" (*Lucae ultimo
capite*, the last chapter of Luke), instead of the chapter
number, as in book 1.: presumably Fowler just lifted these
from Paynell.

Yet, while sailing in his predecessor's wake, Fowler shows
eagerness to outdo him in correctness and completeness. In
book 2, ch. 9, he alone provides an English version for Mat.
10:36, "A man's own familiar friends are his enemies" (69v),
which More himself in book 2, ch. 16 translates differently:
"The enemies of a man are they that are his own familiars"
(p. 1201G. It is ch. 17 in the other two).

Again in book 2, ch. 9, 2 Tim. 2:5 is quoted very freely
by Tottell, with an unmistakeably Morean simplicity, stream-
lined, as it might be described: "Nemo coronabitur nisi qui
legitime certaverit, there shall no man have the crown but
he that doth his devor (= devoir, or endeavour) therefore,
according to the law of the game" (G5r). Paynell substitutes
the Vulgate "Qui certat in agone non coronabitur nisi legitime certaverit" (1178D), yet he retains More's English,
which is now very unlike More. Had his Latin contained the
verb *certare* twice, More would certainly have preserved the
repetition in his rendering of it. Fowler makes a clumsy and
hardly grammatical combination of the original and the Vulgate: "Qui certat in agone, non coronabitur, nisi qui legitime
certaverit" (70r), and he too retains More's English. When
I say "Vulgate," I mean the received text as it read prior to the
many revisions which have given us the modern Vulgate.
Today, for instance, the Vulgate has *coronatur* in 2 Tim. 2:5,
whereas in the sixteenth century some Bibles must have read
coronabitur, a variant still noted in critical editions.

In book 3, ch. 14, Tottell has: "Que societas lucis ad tenebras? Christo ad Belial? what fellowship is there between light and darkness? between Christ and Belial?" (P7v). A modern editor would be tempted to amend *lucis* to *luci*, assuming that a dative *luci* must have corresponded to the dative *Christo*. Paynell, having found the reference in 2 Cor. 6:14, substitutes the full text: "Quae societas luci ad tenebras? Quae autem conventio Christi ad Belial?" (1228F) As usual he respects More's English, which now looks truncated and inadequate. Fowler too has the complete verse, although he has *lucis* in the first sentence, maybe a misprint, maybe fidelity to a genitive in the original.

A long quotation from Mat. 6:19–21 in book 3, ch. 15 is worth studying in some detail, as the variations are very intriguing: Paynell and Fowler have clearly tampered with both the Latin and the English, yet they have refrained from overhauling the text drastically. Of equal interest would be a thorough collation of two other long texts: I Cor. 2:9 and 2 Cor. 11:23–29. Both occur in the penultimate chapter of the book, which More may have written at greater haste, or overseen with less care. Variants are minute in 2 Cor., for example *perils* versus *peril*, but they are considerable in I Cor., which is obviously wrong and unsatisfactory in all three editions (cf. U6r, 1259C and 208v).

The impression of haste is enhanced by a false ascription in the last chapter. Tottell has "Therefore saith S. Peter, Resistite diabolo et fugiet a vobis. Stand against the devil, and he shall fly from you." This is in fact James 4:7, but it does sound like much that St Peter wrote, and the error is not shameful. Paynell, however, having tracked the reference, duly changes Peter to James, and Fowler follows him in this. They also have *flee*, not *fly*. The two forms were probably much closer at that time than they are now: in More's merry tale of "the Sargeant who would play the friar," we have *frere* rhyming with *officere*, and *fryre* rhyming with *desyre*.

One last instance will enable us to see a fourth editor at work, this time probably using More's autograph. The famous passage in Luke 12:4–5, on f. 66v–67 of the Valencia holograph of the *Passionis Expositio*, reads: "nolite inquit timere eos qui occidu*n*t corpus et post hec no*n* habe*n*t quid ultra possint facere. Ego vobis ostenda*m* que*m* debetis timere. que*m* timeatis Timete eu*m* qui quu*m* occiderit corpus/potestate*m* habet a*n*i*m*am simul mittere in geenna*m* Ita dico uobis hu*n*c timete." More's own hesitation—unless it be sheer unrevised oversight—is shown by the duplication "quem debetis timere. quem timeatis." The 1565 Louvain edition, followed by the 1689 Gensch edition (p. 161, col. I, §. 2), changes this into: "Ne terreamini (inquit) ab his, qui occidunt corpus, et post haec non habent amplius quid faciant. Ostendam autem vobis quem timeatis: Timete eum, qui postquam occiderit corpus, habet potestatem mittere in gehennam. Ita dico vobis, hunc timete." Now this passage occurs twice in book 3 of the *Dialogue*. Only verse 4, however, in ch. 24, where Tottell has: "Nolite timere eos qui corpus possunt occidere, et vlterius non habent quod faciunt [*sic*, maybe for *faciant*]" (T8v). Paynell (1255B) amends this to "Ne terreamini ab his qui occidunt corpus, et posthac non habent amplius quid faciant," which tallies with the Vulgate and with the printed *Passionis Expositio*. Fowler, rather surprisingly, retains "nolite timere," but follows the Vulgate from "qui occidunt" on. In ch. 25 (U3r, 1257A and 204v) the passage is more complete, and would deserve careful collation. My purpose is to show the 1565 editor—perhaps Rastell himself, who died at Louvain while the *Opera Latina* were in the press—handling the scriptural material with no more qualms than the 1557 and 1573 editors. More's holograph treatise may prove invaluable in helping fix many biblical passages quoted in other post-humous writings of his. Where his hand has "Non est species nec decor in vultu ejus" (f. 6), the printed edition has "non est ei species neque decor," as in the Vulgate Isaias (1689 ed.

p. 149 col. I). Where the autograph reads "Si videbas furem currebas cum eo" (f. 7), the editor adds the second hemistich of the verse (Ps. 49:18), "et cum adulteris portionem tuam ponebas" (*ibid.* col. 1.–2). Fairly often, where Mary Bassett has been accused of translating her grandfather's Latin overfreely, she was actually very close to her model, which was More's own copy, although she was far from the printed Latin (see for instance 1362A).

The likelihood of tampering must be in our minds whenever we read any of More's works not published under his personal supervision, including, therefore, the unfinished book 9 of the *Confutation*, the *Four Last Things*, the early poems, and the two treatises written just before his imprisonment. Much new light is sure to be thrown on the *Dialogue of Comfort* through collation of the three Tudor editions with the early manuscripts. There is one at Corpus Christi College, Oxford, and one at the British Museum. A third one might turn up, since Fowler's manuscript, if he had one, would hardly have been allowed to find its way back from Recusant hands into a hostile England. Fowler and Tottell agree together more often than they do with the folio, not only in points of structure and content, but in their preference for certain forms, such as *afraid* where the folio has *afeard* (2, 11; 2, 13; 2, 16). Yet in 2, 12, Fowler agrees with the folio in having *afeard*. Can we tell from other sources whether More had a preference, and, if so, which of the two forms he liked best? Within a few lines in his early *The Sargeant*, we read: "And he answerde/Be not aferde," then "The sergent said/ Be not afraid."

Not only for scripture, but in other sentences, internal criticism will often reveal the superiority of the drab, unprepossessing Tottell, for example at the end of book 2, ch. 12: "bee it an asse colt, or a lions whelpe, a rocke of stone or a mist" (H2r). This was pitifully mangled in the folio into "be it an asse, colt or a lions whelp or a rocke of stone, or a mist" (1182A), possibly by the printer responsible for the punctuation, and Fowler only partly repaired the damage (76v).

[Because of the author's returning to France by boat in the fall of 1965, two copies of his paper reached the editor, with some variant readings; and the preceding text is a conflation of these two versions—however, there has been no attempt to record variants in an *apparatus criticus*.]
[Except in quotations from More's autograph, the spelling has been modernized whenever it was felt that merely graphic differences might distract the reader's attention from real textual discrepancies.]

PUBLISHER GUILLAUME ROUILLE, BUSINESSMAN AND HUMANIST

Natalie Zemon Davis

VERYONE HAS heard of the sixteenth-century printers Robert Estienne, Sébastien Gryphius, and Jean de Tournes, but the name Guillaume Rouillé is not recognized very often by scholars outside the field of book-illustration. Not so in his own day, when his fellow citizens in Lyon knew well this offspring of a peasant family who acquired enormous wealth, high political office in the city, and the ennoblement which went with it.[1] Not so in Antwerp and Frankfurt, in Medina del Campo and Saragossa, in Venice and Naples, where his publications were regularly sold. Indeed, his book production

---

[1]The basic work on Rouillé is J. Baudrier, *Bibliographie lyonnaise* (Lyon, 1895–1921), vol. IX, which includes a bibliography of his editions. E. Picot has a chapter on him in his *Les français italianisants au XVIe siècle* (Paris, 1906), I, 183–220. Also, Ruth Mortimer's comments on some of his editions in *Harvard College Library Department of Printing and Graphic Arts: Catalogue of Books and Manuscripts* (Cambridge, Mass., 1964), I, are very useful. That Rouillé came from a well-off peasant family in Loches is clear from details given in his testament (Baudrier, IX, 112–13). The rural character of Loches is shown in a 16th-century representation given in P. Lavedan, *Les villes françaises* (Paris, 1960), 68.

For the high esteem in which Rouillé was still held in Lyon in the eighteenth century, see the remarks of the Père Colonia in *Histoire littéraire de la ville de Lyon* (Lyon, 1730), II, 609–10.

exceeded that of Robert Estienne, Gryphius, and de Tournes, and his learning at least equalled theirs. His relative obscurity in the twentieth century may be due to the character of his humanism and to the kind of economic role he played. He is associated neither with critical editions of the classics in Greek and Latin, nor with the French editions of the Pléiade. Furthermore, Rouillé was not a printer at all, but a merchant-publisher.[2] Thus to our industrial society he seems less appealing than publisher-printers like Estienne, with their incipient "factories" and numerous workers.

Merchant-publishers did not own presses or administer a printing shop. Ordinarily they did own ornamental alphabets —Rouillé had several sets— and if they were at all interested in book illustration, they owned many woodcuts and plates. Some merchant-publishers even had their own type, though this was not the case with Rouillé. They all had to get hold of paper, the most expensive single item in sixteenth-century book production. Rouillé managed this by having one of his in-laws buy a paper mill.[3] The merchant-publisher then "put out" his copy, his paper, and his material to a master printer, as a clothier put out his wool to a master weaver, and the master printer contracted to print it by a certain date.[4] Finally, the publisher marketed the books at the fairs of

[2]Miss Mortimer points out that in the first French editions of Guillaume Du Choul's *Discours sur la religion* and *Discours sur la castramentation et discipline militaire* (1557), the phrase "De l'imprimerie de Guillaume Rouillé" appears on the title pages. This is the only time that phrase appears in Rouillé's whole output. There is no documentary evidence showing that he had a shop in those years. See his description of his work on Du Choul's editions in his letter to Lodovico Domenichi in *Dialogo dell'Imprese Militari et Amorose di Monsignor Giovio . . . Con un Raginamento di Messer Lodovico Domenichi nel medesimo soggetto . . .* (Lyon: Rouillé, 1559), a 2^r (Newberry). No mention is made there of a printing shop.

[3]Baudrier, IX, 80 (act of May 7, 1552). On the expense of paper and other economic aspects of printing, see the excellent discussion of L. Febvre and H. J. Martin, *L'apparition du livre* (Paris, 1958), chaps. 7, 8. [Mme Veyrin-Forrer, Bibliothèque Nationale, informed me, when this article was in proof, of evidence that Rouillé ordered punches and matrices in 1550.]

[4]In Lyon when a master printer was late in his work, he was charged "interest" by the publishers (Bibl. nat., Nouv. acquis. fr. 8014, p. 700).

Frankfurt and Lyon, and wherever else he had commercial contacts. He was also likely to sell books produced by other publishers, as Rouillé, for instance, sold those printed in Antwerp by Christophe Plantin.[5]

When Rouillé, as a young man, arrived in Lyon around 1543, he was in a position to choose between the economic roles of publisher-printer and merchant-publisher. He had just come from Venice where he had apprenticed with Giovanni Giolito and his son Gabriello. During those very years, the Giolito had added a printing shop to their earlier business of bookselling and publishing.[6] Thus Rouillé had been trained in both the commercial and industrial sides of publishing. It is not hard to imagine why he made the choice he did. To be a really successful publisher-printer, you need not only to get hold of a large supply of capital, but also to keep all your presses going by a steady flow of copy and a staff of obedient journeymen. If this was achieved—and it was in the dazzling case of Christophe Plantin with his total of almost 2,000 editions[7]—a very efficient use of machines and labour was possible. But not many men had Plantin's combination of skills in accounting and marketing, in acquiring imperial monopolies for lucrative editions, and in dealing with workers.[8] Furthermore, the situation in Lyon in the early 1540's would have put even a Plantin to the test.

[5]*Correspondance de Christophe Plantin*, ed. M. Rooses and J. Denucé in *Maatschappij der Antwerpsche Bibliophilen*, XII (1883), 47–8.

[6]S. Bongi, *Annali di Gabriel Giolito de'Ferrari da Trino di Monferrato, Stampatore in Venezia* (Rome, 1890–93), xx–xxvi; F. Ascarelli, *La tipografia cinquecentina Italiana* (Florence, 1953), 190–91. Baudrier (IX, 18) got the date of Giovanni's death wrong (he died in late 1539 or early 1540, not in 1542) and did not report the entrance of the Giolito firm into printing.

[7]Colin Clair, *Christophe Plantin* (London, 1960), 216.

[8]See Raymond de Roover, "The Business Organization of the Plantin Press in the Setting of Sixteenth-Century Antwerp," *Gedenkboek der Plantin-Dagen, 1555–1955* (Antwerp, 1956), 230–46 and Robert Kingdon, "Patronage, Piety, and Printing in Sixteenth-Century Europe," in *A Festschrift for Frederick B. Artz* (North Carolina, 1964), 19–36. I have also had profitable discussions with Professor de Roover and Mr. James Wells on the reasons for Plantin's success. For the significance of Plantin's

Specifically, Rouillé would have observed in 1543 that printers' journeymen of Lyon had recently put on an industry-wide strike and that they were even then involved in litigation with their masters. When labour trouble was in the offing, Rouillé must have been unwilling to open a printing shop.[9]

In addition, he was breaking into a field in which Sébastien Gryphius was already well-established as a humanist publisher-printer (not to mention several lesser printers) and in which the major merchant-publishers of Lyon had organized themselves into the Grande Compagnie des Libraires, a permanent partnership for the publication of profitable texts in civil and canon law.[10] In this competitive situation, Rouillé wanted the freedom to expand or cut down the master printers working for him as his supply of copy grew or diminished.

Finally, Rouillé could have readily noticed that the big money and high social prestige in Lyon went to the merchant-publishers, not to the publisher-printers. The tax lists of 1545 estimate the wealth of Luxembourg de Gabiano of the Grande Compagnie des Libraires at twice that of Gryphius. And Gabiano and his partners were often called to the town consulate, while the learned Gryphius never was.[11] He was

---

labour policy, see my article "A Trade Union in Sixteenth-Century France," *Economic History Review*, 2nd. series, XIX (1966).

[9]H. Hauser, *Ouvriers du temps passé* (Paris, 1927), chap. X gives the story of this strike. Some new materials are added by Paul Chauvet in *Les ouvriers du livre en France des origines à la Révolution* (Paris, 1959), 19–43. Both Etienne Dolet and Jean de Tournes set up their printing shops during the strike or litigation. Both of them were close friends at least of one leader of the journeymen's "Company," namely, Vincent Pillet. As I have suggested in greater detail in my forthcoming book *Strikes and Salvation at Lyons*, both men must have opened their shops with policies favourable to the demands of the journeymen's Company.

[10]See Baudrier VII, 26–8.

[11]Archives Communales de Lyon, CC41, Gabiano at 600 *livres* (3ʳ); Gryphius at 300 *livres* (10ʳ, the highest of any master printer in Lyon); Rouillé already at 100 *livres* (5ᵛ) as compared with, say, 80 *livres* for Thibaud Payen (6ᵛ), a publisher-printer of more than fifteen years standing. The merchant-publishers who became consuls in the period up to 1560 were various members of the following families: Gabiano, Vincent, La Porte, and Senneton.

just an artisan. Thus if Rouillé had had any ambition or
devotion to the humanist ideal of civic service it would have
pushed him toward the role of merchant-publisher.

So Rouillé set himself up in business in 1545 under the
Sign of Venice. Newcomer though he was, he marshalled
much capital right away. He married the daughter of Vincent
de Portunariis, an Italian merchant-publisher in Lyon, whose
business was declining, but whose name and contacts were
still good. Cousin Mathieu back home in the Touraine sent
what he could. A certain financial officer made him an enormous long-term loan—16,500 *livres*.[12] Since the Grande Compagnie des Libraires was not willing to take him in, he cut
down on his risks by short-term partnerships for specific editions.[13] In his first year Rouillé published eight works; five
years later he was to publish forty-six.[14]

Other merchant-publishers might boast that yearly output,
but few of them could match Rouillé's involvement in the
editing, illustrating, and correcting, even in the writing of his
editions. Rouillé had learning and he had taste. His training
in Venice had brought him close to every aspect of book-
production, a practical education had by few members of the
Grande Compagnie des Libraires. Moreover, his short-term
partnerships in Lyon were as likely to be with the masters who
were printing his works as with other merchant-publishers—

[12]Baudrier, IX, 20, 82, 112–13. Rouillé's marriage into the Portunariis
family was surely facilitated by the fact that decades before Giovanni
Giolito, Rouillé's master, had had a short-term partnership with Portunariis
(Bongi, I, xvi).

[13]Short-term partnerships, for instance, with Macé Bonhomme (for
the Alciati *Emblems* especially), Thibaud Payen, Antoine Constantin,
Jean de Tournes, Claude La Ville, Etienne Groulleau of Paris, Gabriello
Giolito at Venice, his nephew Philippe Gautier Rouillé at Paris. In the
1560's and after, he had short-term partnerships with certain members of
the Grande Compagnie, such as Philippe Tinghi (Baudrier, IX, 22–3 and
passim).

[14]I here put together the editions given in Baudrier with the ones that
I have found which he did not know (see appendix). All totals in this
paper will include newly found editions.

a device which must have increased his control over the quality of his publications.[15]

That control was exercised for forty-five years and resulted in more than 830 editions.[16] Let us turn to these editions. First we will look at what kinds of books he published and then try to understand what business or personal considerations led to his publication policy.

More than 13 per cent of Rouillé's editions were literary, but hardly any of them were written by his fellow-countrymen. Marot was the only French poet to whom he paid much attention.[17] In contrast, he published Dante's *Commedia*, Boccaccio's *Decameron*, Petrarch's *Sonnets*, Castiglione's *Courtier*, and Ariosto's *Orlando Furioso*. He published them not once, but many times. Boccaccio he had translated into French and Ariosto into French and Italian. In addition Rouillé put out numerous editions of emblem books composed by Italians: those of the celebrated jurist Andrea Alciati, Paolo Giovio, Ludovico Domenichi, and Gabriello Simeoni. Here the works appeared in several languages—Italian, French, and Spanish,

[15]One of the founding members of the Grande Compagnie, Luxembourg I de Gabiano, had worked in the Aldine shop in Venice, and had a training in the industrial and commercial sides of publishing, but most of Rouillé's contemporaries in the Compagnie had not. Thibaud Payen and Antoine Gryphius sold their presses in the 1560's and became *libraires* only. It would be interesting to examine their work as publishers for the effect on it of their previous experience as printers.

Rouillé's partnerships with master printers, such as Bonhomme, are characteristic of his business practice up to about 1560. After that date, he is more likely to make arrangements with other publishers.

[16]As compared with somewhat over 500 editions for publisher-printers Robert Estienne, Sébastien Gryphius, and Jean I de Tournes. On Estienne's career, see the excellent study of Elizabeth Armstrong, *Robert Estienne, Royal Printer* (Cambridge, 1954). Rouillé averaged about 18 editions per year for his whole 45 years of publishing, with an average of 26 editions per year during the years 1548 through 1567. In contrast, Christophe Plantin's yearly average was 45 editions; and Robert Estienne's average, during his 25 years in Paris, was about 18, while it fell to 6 volumes per year when he moved to Geneva (Armstrong, 27).

[17]Baudrier, IX, 129, 146, 179, 192, 209, 217, 249. Rouillé also did an edition of Bonaventure des Périers, a few of Marguerite de Navarre, and some poems by the minor figure Guillaume de La Tayssonière.

and for Alciati, also the original Latin.[18] Italians such as Ficino figured too in Rouillé's small collection of recent philosophical and moral writings.[19]

The literary, historical, and philosophical writings of antiquity, a mainstay of the business of Aldus Manutius and Sébastien Gryphius, made up only about 5 per cent of Rouillé's output. Cicero, for instance, is represented in Latin only by little sentences excerpted from his work.[20] Rouillé did publish a few good textbooks for learning Greek and a Greek-Latin dictionary, but virtually no books in Greek to use them on. He seems to have preferred his Greek authors in French, as in a fine translation of Herodianus' *History of the Roman Emperors.*[21]

[18]See Picot's discussion of Rouillé's Italian editions, *op. cit.* These editions of Italian literature and emblem-books are readily available in American and Canadian rare-book collections. I have found them at the University of Toronto, the Toronto Public Library, the Newberry Library, the Folger Library, the Houghton Library of Harvard University, the New York Public Library, and the University of Michigan Library. Rouillé also published Paterno's *Il Nuove Fiamme* (1568, U. of Toronto) and produced works of literary criticism, such as Ridolfi's *Ragionamento* on Boccaccio (1557, U. of Toronto) and the 1573 Latin commentary on Alciati's *Emblems* by the Spaniard Francisco Sanchez de las Brozas (U. of Toronto).

[19]*Marsilii Ficino Florentini Medici atque Philosophi celeberrimi, De Vita Libri tres* (1566, Western Reserve). Rouillé also published Marguérite de Cambis' translations of Boccaccio's *Letter of Consolation* (1556, Houghton) as well as a translation from the Spanish made by Marguérite's husband Jacques de Rochemore—Guevara's *Favory de Court* (1556, Houghton). Another work in this category is the Neoplatonic *Philosophy of Love*, written in the 16th century by "Leon the Jew" (Judah Abrabanel) and translated from Italian into French for Rouillé by Denis Sauvage (1551 ed., N.Y. Public and Columbia).

[20]*M. Tul. Ciceronis Sententiae Insigniores . . . Omnia Petri Lagnerii Compeniensis opera congesta . . . Quibus accesserunt P. Terentii insigniores sententiae*, 1555 (Newberry, not in Baudrier). Rouillé also published editions of Catullus (1559, Columbia) and Horace (1574, Columbia), but neither of these works first appeared under his mark. The one classical edition which he may have helped initiate is Denis Lambin's translation of Lucretius (1563, U. of Toronto; 1564, Columbia); but this work he published with his nephew in Paris, as a means of getting him established there.

[21]*Clenardi Grammaticae Institutiones Graecae* and *Clenardi Meditationes Graecae in artem grammaticam* (both 1546, Newberry, not in Baudrier); also Baudrier, IX, 244, 308. There is some Greek in his editions of Hippocrates. *L'Histoire d'Herodian, Excellent Historiographe, Traitant de la*

RAGIONAMEN-
TO HAVVTO IN LIO-
NE DA CLAVDIO DE
HERBERE', GENTIL'HVO-
MO FRANZESE,

ET DA ALESSANDRO DE
GLIVBERTI, GENTIL'HVOMO
FIORENTINO, SOPRA ALCVNI
LVOGHI DEL CENTO
NOVELLE DEL
BOCCACCIO.

ALESSANDRO.

A M E (*Claudio*) *veramente pare, che
quel tempo che da noi fiete flato lon-
tano, voi fiate dimorato in quella Cit
tà, oue & per dono di natura, & per
lo diligēte ftudio, piu ornatamēte che
in alcuna dell'altre; è da i piu intēdē
ti giudicato, che quefta lingua fi par
li, & nõ alla Corte & à Parigi, co-
me dite hauer fatto: dapoi che (lafciato hora à parte il voftro na
tio idioma Frãzefe) m'hauete in quefto rifpofto, correttamēte
fempre fauellãdo: cofa che di voi, nel vero, m'è giũta inafpettata
molto.* CLAV. *Io pure, Aleffandro, come hor vi diceua, fono
flato tra la Corte & Parigi, due anni & mezzo; che tanti fono à pũto da che di qui di Lione mi partij; ad hoggi hà otto gior*

A 2

While such classical historians were few in Rouillé's inventory, works by recent or contemporary historians appeared frequently, about fifty-six editions in all. Among the most significant was his own *Promptuary of Medallions*. Appearing in Latin, French, Italian, and Spanish, it presented medallions and biographies of prehistorical and historical figures from Adam to his own day.[22] The Lyonnais jurist Guillaume du Choul brought him discourses on the military discipline and religion of the Greeks and Romans, which Rouillé then had illustrated and gave to Europe in several languages.[23] He did contemporary histories and urban histories and accounts of travel to the Near East, such as Nicolas de Nicolay's *Pérégrinations Orientales* among the Turks.[24] Indeed, for several years Rouillé had the skilful royal historiographer Denis Sauvage

---

vie des Successeurs de Marc Aurele à l'Empire de Romme: Translatee de Greq en Françoys par Jaques des Contes de Vintemille, Rhodien, edition shared with Jean de Tournes (1554, Pierpont Morgan). Similarly, another of the classical editions in which Rouillé really took an interest is in French: *Trois premiers livres de la metamorphose d'Ovide, Traduictz en vers Francois: Le premier et second par Cl. Marot, Le tiers par B. Aneau* (1556, Houghton).

[22]Of the 11 editions which Rouillé published of this work (four in French, three each in Latin and Italian, and one in Spanish) the Newberry Library has several; and the New York Public Library, the Houghton Library, and Brown University have French editions.

[23]Eleven editions, most of which include both the military and the religious *Discourses*: five in French (Newberry has 1555, *Castramentation* and 1556, *Religion*; Houghton has the 1557 editions) and one in Spanish (1579, Houghton).

[24]For instance, *Historia di Pietro Bizari Della guerra fatta in Ungheria dall' invittissimo Imperatore de Christiani, contra quello de Turchii, Con la narratione di tutte quelle cose che sono auvenute in Europa, dall'anno 1564 in sino all' anno 1568* (1568, John Carter Brown; 1569, Newberry); *Discours Historial de l'antique et illustre cité de Nismes en la Gaule Narbonoise . . . par Jean Poldo d'Albenas* (1560, Newberry); *Les quatres premiers livres des Navigations et Pérégrinations Orientales de N. de Nicolay . . . Avec les figures au naturel tant d'hommes que de femmes* (1568, Houghton). Rouillé published in 1561 and 1562 the geographical-historical studies of Constantinople (Newberry) and the Bosporus (Houghton) by Pierre Gilles written in Latin. In the category of "news" one could include Rouillé's editions in French and Italian of the Entry of Henri II in Lyons (1549 Italian *Entrata* at Houghton).

working for him, editing historical manuscripts from the late medieval period and translating other works from the Italian.[25]

Books in law and medicine account for about 40 per cent of Rouillé's publications. Most of the legal books concern

DISTRIBUTION OF ROUILLÉ'S PUBLICATIONS BY SUBJECT
AND LANGUAGE

Subject	Latin	Vernaculars (Fr., It., Sp.)		Total	Percentage of total editions
Classics (literary, philosophical, historical)	34	7		41	4.9
Literary and Language (non-classical poetry, drama, emblems, etc.)	23	87		110	13.2
Recent philosophy, etc. (Neoplatonism, love, logic, education)	18	16		34	4.1
History (works by recent or contemporary writers, including travel, geography)	8	48		56	6.7
Law	180*	3		183	22.0
Civil law	145		3		
Canon law	35		0		
Medicine	146	3		149	17.8
Other Science (surgery, pharmacy, botany, etc.)	42	25		67	8.0
Religion	157	37		194	23.2
Bibles, Bible pictures	16		29		
Theology, doctrine	132		3		
Missals, hours	9		5		
TOTAL	608	226		834	—

*In three cases, a single legal "edition" is actually a work of ten or more volumes.

[25]Sauvage's first work for Rouillé occurred in 1550, his last in 1562 (Baudrier, IX, 177, 291). His editions include a translation of Paolo Giovio's *Histories* (2nd ed. 1558, Pierpont Morgan); *Cronique des Flandres, Ancienement Composee par Auteur Incertain et nouvellement mise en lumiere par Denis Sauvage* (1562, N.Y. Public); *Continuation de l'Histoire et Cronique de Flandres, Extraitte de plusieurs bons Auteurs, par Denis Sauvage* (1561, N.Y. Public); and *Les Memoires de Messire Olivier de La Marche . . . Nouvellement mis en lumiere par Denis Sauvage* (1562,

civil rather than canon law.[26] They are not the bulky editions
with commentaries by the old Italian glossators and post-
glossators, that were usually published by the Grande Compagnie des Libraires.[27] Rouillé's *Corpus juris civilis* came in
convenient sextodecimo volumes, "hand editions" as Rouillé
would say. And his commentators were ordinarily French
contemporaries—Tiraqueau, Coras, Duaren, Cujas—followers,
in varying degrees, of the new school of humanist jurisprudence which argued that Roman law had to be studied
with the tools of history and philology.[28] This literature was,
of course, in Latin. Rouillé did not publish French edicts,

N.Y. Public). For the last three Sauvage transcribed the manuscript,
modernized the spelling, and added punctuation and chapter divisions.
He also contributed marginal comments and annotations to explain archaic
phrases and obscure events.

On Sauvage, see E. Droz, "Notes sur Théodore de Bèze," *Bibliothèque
d'humanisme et renaissance*, XXIV (1962), 609–10 and Natalie Z. Davis,
"Peletier and Beza Part Company," *Studies in the Renaissance*, XI (1964),
212–13.

[26]Of Rouillé's thirty-five editions in canon law, twenty-two were published
after 1570. He published one edition of the *Corpus juris canonici*, 1555
(Baudrier, IX, 219). Copies of the *Sextus Decretalium Liber: Per Boni-
facium Octavum Pontificem . . . . editus* (N.Y. Public) and the *Decreta*
of Gratian (Pierpont Morgan) were bought by Pietro Duodo, Venetian
ambassador to France in the 1590's. Both copies are beautifully bound.

[27]Baudrier, IX, 31. There are, to be sure, commentaries by Hotman,
Zasius, and Du Moulin published by partners in the Compagnie (331,
336, 408, 429), but on the whole it was the "mos italicus" or traditional
school which the Compagnie published. The Compagnie's willingness to
publish less traditional commentaries in the 1550's and 1560's may be a
response to Rouillé's success, though religious considerations may be relevant. Among Rouillé's own publications, the "mos italicus" is represented
by three editions of the *Tractatus de indiciis et Tortura* by Francesco
Bruno, Guido de Suzaria, and others (1547, Newberry).

[28]On humanist jurisprudence, see Myron P. Gilmore, *Argument from
Roman Law in Political Thought, 1200–1600* (Cambridge, Mass., 1941),
chaps. 1–2 and *Humanists and Jurists, Six Studies in the Renaissance*
(Cambridge, Mass., 1963), 28–37; Linton Stevens, "The Contribution of
French Jurists to the Humanism of the Renaissance," *Studies in the
Renaissance*, I (1954), 92–105; Guido Kisch, "Humanist Jurisprudence"
Studies in the Renaissance, VIII (1961), 71–87.

I have found Rouillé's editions in civil law at the Newberry, Houghton,
Columbia, and the University of Michigan. The Harvard Law School alone
has forty-eight of his editions in civil law, including some not in Baudrier
(see appendix), as well as a few more on canon law.

laws, and town cries, while eloquent French *plaidoyers*, which might have interested him, did not begin until after his death.[29]

The medical editions sold from the shop at the Sign of Venice were almost as numerous as the legal ones. Mostly they were Latin editions of Galen, "hand editions" again, freshly translated and with commentaries by outstanding sixteenth-century physicians—Linacre of England, Cop of Basel, Sylvius of France, Leonicus of Italy, and so on.[30] As in the case of jurisprudence, Rouillé's publications expressed the current humanist view in medicine, which favoured Galen over Hippocrates and expressed the need for translations and interpretations freed from the "corruptions" of the Arabs —preferences for which, incidentally, modern historians of medicine have not always had praise.[31] Original works by humanist-physicians also appeared under Rouillé's mark, such as those by his friend and collaborator Jacques Dalechamps.[32]

Nor did Rouillé limit his scientific publications to medicine.

[29]For legal editions in French, see Baudrier, IX, 209–10, 241, 315–316. On judicial eloquence in the vernacular, see Catherine Holmes' thesis, shortly to be published, *L'eloquence judicaire de 1620 à 1660.*

[30]For the first twenty years of his publishing career, Rouillé's editions in medicine outnumbered those in law. I have found Rouillé's medical editions at the Toronto Academy of Medicine, at the Houghton Library (three editions of Galen, 1548–1550, bound together for Marcus Fugger), Columbia, and the University of Michigan Medical Center Library (see appendix). Undoubtedly there are many more in the medical library in Boston and at the Academy of Medicine in New York.

[31]W. P. D. Wightman, *Science and the Renaissance* (Edinburgh, 1962) I, 211–13. For instance, Rouillé pointed out in his preface to Galen's *De morborum et symptomatum differentiis et causis libri sex*, with annotations by Guillaume Cop (1550, Houghton), that the text had been restored according to authentic Greek codices, partly from the annotations of Agostino Ricci of Lucca, partly by the judgment of learned physicians. "Thus, those who do not know Greek or have trouble with it can read the true mind of Galen." Hippocrates, though receiving less attention than Galen, was not totally ignored. Rouillé, for instance, published in 1577 an important Latin edition of Hippocrates, with commentaries by Jacques Houlier and edited by Desideré Iacot (Columbia).

[32]Baudrier, IX, 196. Rouillé also published Guillaume Rondelet's *Methodus curandorum* (1576, U. of Aberdeen, originally owned by the 16th-century scientist Duncan Liddell; 1586, Toronto Academy of Medicine).

He was happy to bring out recent works on surgery by Jean Tagault and others.[33] He published a few works in pure and applied mathematics[34] and several French editions of the *Secrets of Alexis of Piedmont*, a manual of recipes for everything from tooth-paste to textile dyes. He was especially interested by botany and pharmacology. His illustrated editions in these fields included those works that most encouraged observation and systematization:[35] Dioscorides and Theophrastus in Latin translations; Matthioli's important commentaries translated into French; a folio edition of Dalechamps' *Historia Generalis Plantarum*. For this last work Rouillé had his friends send him plant specimens from all over the world.[36]

Rouillé's publications concerning the next world, however, were much less numerous than those concerning the present one. They make up less than one quarter of his editions. That he published few of the scholastic theologians is not surprising, but where are the critical editions of the Church Fathers which had so interested Erasmus and other Christian humanists?[37]

---

[33]E.g., Tagault's *De chirurgica Institutione libri quinque* (1549 and 1587, U. of Mich. Medical Center); *Chirurgie françoise recueillie par M. Iaques Dalechamps* (1570, N.Y. Public). In all he published 10 editions on surgery.

[34]Specifically, the *Logistica* (U. of Mich., Columbia) and *De Quadratura circuli* (U. of Wisc., N.Y. Public) of Jean Borrel, alias Bueot, and Medina's *Art of Navigation*, translated from Spanish into French by Nicolas de Nicolay (1554 and 1569, John Carter Brown).

[35]Whitman, I, 185–7, 195, 197.

[36]*Historia Generalis Plantarum in Libros XVIII* (1587, Cleveland Medical, N.Y. Public), to the reader, 3ʳ–4ᵛ. Dioscorides' *de Medica Materia* was first printed and published by Balthazar Arnoullet in 1552. Rouillé's 1558 edition (Cleveland Medical) is simply a copy of this edition, printed by Arnoullet's widow. A French translation of Matthioli, made by Antoine du Pinet and printed by Gabriel Cotier, had first appeared in Lyon in 1561, but Matthioli himself had criticized its accuracy in the preface to the Venice 1565 edition of the work. Even before 1565 Rouillé sponsored a new translation: *Commentaires de M. Pierre Andre Matthiole, Medecin Senois sur les six livres de Ped. Dioscor. Anazarbien de la Matiere Medicinale . . . Mis en François sur la derniere edition Latine de l'Autheur, par M. Iean des Moulins Docteur en Medicine* (1572; 1578 ed. N.Y. Public), a 2ʳ -a 3ᵛ.

[37]His few scholastic editions are: Durandus' commentaries on Lombard's *Sentences* (1563, Union Theological Seminary, with slightly different

As there were no polemics among his political books, so there were almost none among his religious books. But why are there so few serious discussions of free will, justification, and church polity? The name of the unexceptionable Franciscan Francis Titelmann appears often in Rouillé's inventory; so does that of the little-known preacher Joannes Ferus (Johann Wild) of Mainz.[38] But Calvin's name hardly ever appears, in any context up to 1561, and after that it is most likely to be found in the Indexes of Prohibited Books which he published in his later decades.[39] There are no Huguenot Psalters; there are some missals and a few beautifully decorated Books of Hours (including one in Spanish),[40] but no other popular vernacular works of consolation and piety. And yet there is after all one strong link between Rouillé's publications and the great religious controversy of his century: his many Bibles and Bible pictures. The former were in Latin, French, and

---

colophon from Baudrier, IX, 292) and late in his career works of Aquinas and Nicolas de Lyra (*ibid.*, 327–8, 392, 407). Though Rouillé published some excerpts from Augustine (1580, N.Y. Public) his only real edition of the Fathers is the *Opera* of Dionysius the Areopagite (1585, Newberry). On the importance of humanist editions of the Fathers in France, see Eugene Rice, "The Humanist Idea of Christian Antiquity: Lefèvre d'Etaples and his Circle," *Studies in the Renaissance*, IX (1962), 126–60.

[38]Rouillé's editions of Titelmann's theological works and commentaries on the Bible begin in the 1540's (see appendix). He also published Titelmann's writings on logic and natural philosophy. A native of Hasselt, Belgium, Titelmann taught at Louvain. In 1550, his university included his dialectical writings in a short list of works which it was safe to use in teaching school children (H. Reusch, *Die Indices Librorum Prohibitorum* Tübingen, 1886, 71). A few of the works of Ferus found their way to the finicky Spanish lists of books to be expurgated (*ibid.*, 413), but were corrected for the edition of 1569. Most of Ferus' works are commentaries on different parts of the Bible.

[39]For the few polemical works Rouillé published, see *infra* 97 and n. 76. From 1564 to 1588 Rouillé put out six editions of the Index, the first one in a separate edition (Houghton, not in Baudrier), the others as part of the Canons and Decrees of Trent (1572, Newberry).

[40]*Las horas de nuestra señora segū el uso romano*, 1551, edition shared with Macé Bonhomme, who printed the work (Houghton, Mortimer 311; John Carter Brown). The edition was condemned in 1559 on an index drawn up by the Spaniard Valdes (Reusch, 235), but the John Carter Brown copy was in Spanish hands and bears the inscription "visto y aprobado por el p^do Sr Silvestro Pardo."

Italian; the pictures and poems illustrating episodes from the Old and New Testaments were in French and Italian.[41]

Thus the main themes of Rouillé's publications: Italian literature, emblem books, a small number of classical editions, humanist textbooks in civil law and medicine, botanical and surgical writings, and, out of an undistinguished miscellany of religious publications, a line of Bibles and Bible pictures. The rationale for this pattern is found in a combination of business, intellectual, and religious interests.

In the first place, the diversity of Rouillé's publications was simply good business practice. Big merchants had long hedged their risks by dealing in many different wares. Indeed, Christophe Plantin went farther than Rouillé and dealt in maps, astronomical instruments, and other merchandise.[42]

Secondly, Rouillé had a clear idea of what markets he had a good chance of selling to. "There is a dearth of books in the Spanish kingdoms, especially well-corrected ones," he said to the readers of his Spanish edition of Alciati's *Emblems*, "I want to serve you. . . ."[43] So he sent his brothers-in-law to live in Spain and sponsored Spanish translations for them to sell. It was to the Spaniards that he was selling all those books by Francis Titelmann; and it was mostly for their

[41]See *infra*, 95, on these editions. North American copies include a 1551 Latin New Testament (Union Theological Seminary, not in Baudrier), a 1552 Italian New Testament (Newberry), a 1554 French New Testament (N.Y. Public), a 1558 Italian New Testament (Newberry, Houghton), and a 1566 *Biblia Sacra* (Columbia, Newberry, Toronto Public). Houghton has the 1564 *Figures de la Bible*, with verses by Guéroult, the 1565 Italian *Figure de la Biblia* with verses by Simeoni (sometimes translated from Guéroult), and the 1579 *Figures du Nouveau Testament*, with verses by Claude de Pontoux.

[42]Clair, 197–8. On diversification, see Raymond de Roover, *The Rise and Decline of the Medici Bank* (Cambridge, Mass., 1964), 142–3. By the mid 1550's, Rouillé had begun to invest in urban real estate and in the next decade owned five different properties in Lyon. Possibly he sold wine retail (Baudrier, ix, 81–3, 87–8, 123).

[43]*Los Emblemas de Alciato Traducidos en rhimas Espanolas*, 1549 (U. of Toronto), 3; Guillielmo Rouillio librero à los lettores. Copy owned by a Spaniard of Toledo, 1566.

benefit that he enticed copy from the distinguished Spanish theologian Martin Azpilcueta Navaro. Rouillé was not the only Lyonnais merchant to ship books to Spain, but he did very well nevertheless.[44]

Though he entertained the notion of selling some of his Spanish books in France itself, it was with his editions of Italian literature that the merchant at the Sign of Venice intended to attract Franch buyers. Many Frenchmen, Rouillé said, have learned Italian in the course of war, study, or business.[45] Judging from his dedications, I think Rouillé was also counting on their wives to buy.[46] Furthermore, he was living in Lyon, whose large Italian business community had become increasingly interested in letters.[47] Of course, he could not have expected to make huge profits in Italy, where his former master Giolito among others was publishing the same thing. But in France only Jean de Tournes would be a possible competitor.[48] To increase sales, Rouillé brought out his Italian

[44]On Rouillé's business with Spain, see Baudrier, IX, 23, 85–6, 92, 236 and H. Lapeyre, *Une Famille de marchands: Les Ruiz* (Paris, 1955), 567–8, 594. Rouillé's letter to Navaro, dated 16 Calends January, 1573, in *Francisci Sanctii Brocensis . . . Comment. in And. Alciati emblemata*, 1573 (U. of Toronto), 3–4.

[45]*Orlando Furioso de M. Ludovico Ariosto, Traduzido en Romance Castel. por el S. Don Hieronimo de Urrea*, 1556 (U. of Toronto), α2r. Though he also mentions here Frenchmen who knew Spanish, it is clear from his letter to the readers in the 1550 Spanish edition of this poem, 4 (Houghton) and in the 1561 Spanish version of Domenichi's *Emblems* v (Houghton) that he was aiming his Spanish books at the Spanish.

[46]For instance, his dedication of the 1555 Italian Boccaccio and the 1558 Italian Petrarch to Marguérite de Bourg, dame de Gage, wife of a French financial officer. The 1556 *Orlando Furioso* was dedicated to Madame de Termes.

[47]See, for instance, the account of meetings between Italian literary men and Luccan business men at the Arnolfini residence in Lyon in the early 1560's in *Bartholomaei Facii de Rebus Gestis . . . Commentatiorum Libri Decem I. Michaelis Bruti opera . . . editi* (Lyon: heirs Gryphius, 1562), II 1r.

[48]Picot, 160–182 for the modest number of Italian editions published by de Tournes. Rouillé boasts about the convenient size of his Italian editions in the dedications of the 1550 Petrarch, 4 (Houghton) and of the 1558 Petrarch, 5–9 (Houghton).

editions in "hand size," as Aldus Manutius decades before had given small format to the classics.[49]

In legal and medical publishing, where many firms were active, Rouillé tried to get a foothold by catching the student buyers. Not only was he following the new humanist line, but also, as he pointed out in his letters to the reader, he was giving them books that they could easily carry around.[50] With his surgical publications, Rouillé hoped to win students, even apprentices, by publishing in French. He went out looking for translations and, as he said in a letter to students of surgery, finally talked a physician in Paris into converting Jean Tagault's *de Chirurgica institutione* into French. His few French editions of Galen were also addressed "to students of surgery," while he described his edition of Dalechamp's *Chirurgie Françoise* as "for the benefit of journeymen and master Surgeons who have not been brought up in Greek and Latin letters."[51]

Rouillé's success with these editions suggests an interesting feature of his business policy. In an excellent article, Robert Kingdon has concluded that the humanist publications of Henri Estienne and Christophe Plantin "were subsidized either by the generous patronage of men of power or by profits gained by catering to the popular thirst for religious consola-

[49]See the letter to the reader in his *Magni Hippocratis Coaca Praesagia*, in which he explains that since this volume is already bulky, he will eliminate Iacot's commentaries from it and publish them in a small, convenient volume which can be carried around by medical students 1575, ***4r (Columbia). Also, see his letter introducing Galen's *De Morborum et symptomatum differentiis et causis libri sex*, 1550, 3–4 (Houghton).

[50]Baudrier, IX, 166, 225. *De l'usage des parties du corps humain, Livres XVIII, Escripts par Claude Galien*, 1565 (U. Montréal). The translator stressed the usefulness of the book to surgeons (9v), but dedicated the work to a woman. The Montréal copy had a female owner in the 16th century. Rouillé's editions of Plutarch and Boccaccio in French were also aimed at women.

[51]*Chirurgie Francoise, Recueillie par M. Iaques Dalechamps, Docteur Medecin et Lectuer ordinaire de ceste profession à Lyon*, 1570, 7v (U. of Montréal, N.Y. Public: Mr. Wilson Duprey has kindly described for me the New York copy).

tion."[52] Now we have seen that Rouillé published little popular religious literature. In his case, then, legal and scientific
textbooks were the major way he paid for his expensive illustrated editions. In his several editions of *The Secrets of Alexis
of Piedmont* he seems to have been experimenting to the same
end with a do-it-yourself manual.

On Rouillé's methods of seeking patronage, such as his
dedications to Catherine de Medici and other rulers,[53] I
cannot elaborate now. He also used advertising techniques to
increase his sales, the most novel of which was his own widely
read *Promptuary of Medallions*. There he included among
his celebrities the pictures and biographies of authors he was
publishing, often mentioning his own editions explicitly.[54]

Rouillé's publication pattern cannot be explained, however,
only in terms of business decisions and sales strategy. After
all, if he had just wanted to make money, he could have
published the kind of vernacular occasional literature which
appealed to the "mass" French market. Benoît Rigaud, another
peasant's son in Lyon, made his fortune that way. But the
audience which Rouillé was trying to reach, though an international one, was socially more restricted. Except for the

[52]"Patronage, Piety, and Printing in Sixteenth-Century Europe," in *A
Festschrift for Frederick B. Artz* (North Carolina, 1964), 36. In a letter
of October, 1965, Professor Kingdon agrees that my interpretation of
Rouillé's publishing policy is a likely one and adds that popular non-
religious manuals were often used to subsidize scholarly publication.

[53]For instance, the 1553 Latin edition of the *Promptuary of Medallions*
was dedicated to Henri II, the Italian edition to Catherine de Medici, the
French to Marguérite de France, Duchess of Berry. The 1561 French
translation of the Giovio and Domenichi *Emblems* were dedicated to
Catherine. The 1587 *Historia Generalis Plantarum* was dedicated to
Charles Emanuel, Duke of Savoy.

[54]For instance, in the 1577 edition of the French *Promptuaire* (N.Y.
Public), Rouillé mentioned his own editions in the articles on Matthioli,
Donat, Rondelet, Duaren, and Jacques Houlier (263, 269, 271, 274).
See Mrs. Armstrong's discussion of advertising in *Estienne*, 20–26. Rouillé
does not seem to have had a trade catalogue, but, like Robert Estienne,
used his prefaces to announce forthcoming editions. Thus he announced
Houlier's *Commentaries* on Hippocrates in his preface to Rondelet's
Methodus curandorum, which appeared earlier the same year.

Spanish clergy, it was on the whole a lay audience of merchants, professionals, and their wives, of cultivated seigneurs and members of the court. This is the audience of a vernacular humanist with the encyclopedic interests characteristic of the middle decades of the sixteenth century.[55]

Where Rouillé acquired his learning is something of a mystery, since we know little of his movements from his birth in a small town in the Touraine to his arrival in Lyon. There is no sign of his having been to a university. Rather he was educated by his profession and the men he met in the course of it. "I passed many years of my youth in . . . Italy," he tells us, "and learned that language perhaps better than my own."[56] Little wonder that he loved the "purity and sweetness" of the Italian tongue, as he put it later in one of his many Italian prefaces.[57] He got to know Domenichi and Brucioli and other Italian literary figures in Giolito's shop and later had close friends, such as Luca Antonio Ridolfi, in the Italian intellectual circle in Lyon.[58]

Yet he did not forget about "the decoration and augmentation of the French language," as he described the goal of one of his editions.[59] He thought the French language had changed

[55]See Frances A. Yates, *The French Academies of the Sixteenth Century* (London, 1947), chaps. 4–7, for an excellent treatment of the "Renaissance encyclopedia."

[56]Dedicatory letter to Luca Antonio Ridolfi, in *Il Petrarca con nuove et brevi dichiarationi* 1550, 2–4 (Houghton).

[57]Dedication of the *Discorso della Religione antica de Romani, composto in Franzese dal S. Guglielmo Choul*, 1559, 3 (N.Y. Public).

[58]See Bongi's *Annali* for the men frequenting the Giolito shop during Rouillé's years there. Rouillé's friendship with Domenichi is clear from his letter of June 21, 1559 to Domenichi, whom he asks to think of him as "vostro buono amico e fratello" (*Dialogo dell'Imprese Militari et Amorose di Monsignor Giovio . . . Con un Ragionamento di Messer Lodovico Domenichi*, 1559, a 2ʳ⁻ᵛ [Newberry]). Rouillé dedicated one edition of the 1550 Petrarch and the 1552 Dante to Ridolfi. It was mostly at Ridolfi's urging that Rouillé began to publish literary works in Italian. Other Italian friends in Lyon were the Florentine Gabriello Simeoni, the Florentine Baccio Tinghi ("amicissimo mio," Rouillé called him in his 1562 edition of *Il Cortegiano*, 495 [Folger, U. of Michigan]), and the Florentine Francesco Giuntini.

[59]Rouillé's formulation in his request for the privilege for Sauvage's French

much since the days of Louis XII; had become richer, more polished, and sweet. This improvement, to his mind, was due primarily to "good and learned persons . . . who have been translating numerous works from Latin, Greek, and Italian."[60] He was, of course, publishing these translations.

In a general way, most vernacular humanists agreed with Rouillé's position, but how did he stand with regard to the special views of the Pléiade? On the one hand, he published hardly a line of their poetry[61] and *did* publish Marot, whom they were trying to supersede. He employed as editor and translator Barthélemy Aneau, who in the name of French mediaeval verse had let out a great blast against Du Bellay's *Défense et Illustration*. He even published Ariosto's epic in French, thus, for Du Bellay, betraying poetry by translation. On the other hand, Rouillé was the main supplier to the French public of the Italian Petrarch and Ariosto, which the Pléiade adored and imitated. And, poetry aside, Du Bellay and even more Jacques Peletier applauded translations which could enrich the French vocabulary. Thus, the character of Rouillé's vernacular humanism is complex, feeding both the older tradition of Marot and the fashionable work of the Pléiade.[62]

---

translation of the *Histoires de Paolo Iovio* (1558, Pierpont Morgan), privilege dated March 12, 1551 (i.e., 1552).

[60]Baudrier, IX, 37, 182, 248–9.

[61]The only example I have found is a poem by Pontus de Tyard to Jacques de Vintemille in honour of the latter's translation of *Histoire*. This edition was shared, however, with Jean de Tournes, who published several of the works of de Tyard and of Jacques Peletier.

[62]On the quarrel between Aneau and Du Bellay and the views of the Pléiade on translation and the use of Italian poetry, see Henri Chamard, *Histoire de la Pléiade* (Paris, 1939), I, 118–20, 161, 186-88, 206ff.; Bernard Weinberg, *Critical Prefaces of the French Renaissance* (Evanston, 1950), 14–20 and *passim*; and R. J. Clements, *Critical Theory of the Pléiade* (Cambridge, 1942), 261–2. Clements plays down Du Bellay's criticism of translation of poetry.

Aneau states his views on translation in the last part of the preface to the French edition of Alciati's *Emblems* and his preface to the French edition of Ovid's *Metamorphoses*. He defends word for word translation, in opposition to Du Bellay, and says in regard to Ovid, that he has sought French equivalents for antique names "pour ne Graeciser ne Latiniser en

Among the wide interests of his fellow humanists, there
was one, however, which Rouillé did not share. This was
music,[63] of which he never published a note or made mention
in his letters. It can not have been the expense and bother
of musical editions alone which deterred him, for he always
enjoyed complaining about how much time and money he
had put into his illustrated editions.[64] Rather I think he did
not "hear" music at all. What he did have was a highly
developed taste for the visual arts—painting, medallions, which
he collected,[65] and of course woodcuts and engravings. Some
of his publications even began with the illustrations. "It is
twenty years and more," he said in 1586, "since I walked into
the study of the noted physician Jaques Dalechamps and
found him . . . looking at a big volume of pictures of plants."
The sight of these "rare and exquisite pictures" invited
Rouillé to produce the *General History.*[66]

If he could feel so moved by botanical illustrations, we can
easily understand his enthusiasm for the emblem books he
published. "I know well that painting and poetry have a great
affinity," said Rouillé, echoing that cherished humanist view
for which Horace's "ut pictura poesis" was always cited. "The
verses will delight your ears, the pictures nourish your eyes,"
he informed those who bought his Alciati.[67] The publisher

François." The views of Sauvage, who had been a close friend of Peletier in
1547–8, are not precisely those of the Pléiade. In his preface to Abrabanel's
Philosophie d'amour, he explains that he had tried first merely to "paraphrase" the work (as the Pléiade preferred) but this had worked out so
badly that he had started all over again, following the Italian copy word
for word except when the passage was corrupt (8–9).

[63]On the enormous importance of music to humanists, see Yates, *French
Academies,* chaps. 3–4 and Victor E. Graham, "Music for Poetry in France,"
Renaissance News, XVII (1964), 307–17.

[64]For instance, in his preface to the *Figures du Nouveau Testament,
illustrees de huictains francoys,* 1570, Aa 2^v (Houghton).

[65]*Promptuaire des Medalles,* 1553, a 4^r.

[66]*Historia Generalis Plantarum,* 3^r.

[67]*Figures du Nouveau Testament,* Aa 3^r; *Emblemata Andrea Alciati,*
1548, 3 (N.Y. Public). On the theory of emblem literature, see Mario
Praz, *Studies in Seventeenth-Century Imagery* (London, 1939), I, chap. 1
and *passim,* and Robert J. Clements, *Picta Poesis: Literary and Humanistic*

had probably mounted several of these emblems on the walls
and furnishings of his home, for he went on to suggest this
possibility to his readers. "Thus you can give adornment to
the barren things in your house and to the mute things give
words."[68]

Rouillé's preference for botanical works over pure mathematics in his scientific publication is also explained by his
intellectual tastes. Mathematical works are expensive, because
of the problems of display, special figures, and proofreading,
but illustrated botanical works are not cheap either. Rouillé
must have known enough arithmetic for bookkeeping, but
he was no mathematical amateur. In contrast, he often fre-
quented medical circles; and it was in the midst of a chat with
several physicians that he decided finally to publish Matthioli
in French.[69]

The area of Rouillé's publications which is hardest to relate
to his personal interests is the religious. I plan to treat the
religion of Rouillé more fully elsewhere. Here let me assert
that Rouillé was a moderate, not just from humanist convic-
tion, but from prudence; that his religious sensibility was
never deep, at least until he was an old man; and that the
religious position he held was one of simple biblical Christianity, which before 1561 leaned towards, but was never com-
mitted to, the Protestant cause and after that date was com-
mitted to a non-fanatical Catholicism.

Rouillé's first publisher's motto celebrated prudence, and
he was not the only Lyons' publisher to shy away from
dangerous literature under the restraint of that virtue. His
publisher's emblem represented the victory of the eagle over
the snake, a pre-classical symbol which to the mediaeval

Theory in Renaissance Emblem Books (Rome, 1960). Rouillé also thought
of his *Promptuary of Medallions* as satisfying several senses and being, as
emblems were supposed to be, pleasurable and useful: "Cest oeuvre . . .
plaisant à veior en ses figures, delectable à lire, et ouyr en ses escriptures,
profitable en vertueux exemples, recreant l'esprit par diversité et verité
historiale . . . ," *Promptuaire*, 1553, a 2ᵛ.   [68]*Emblemata*, 1548, 3–4.

[69]*Commentaires . . . de Matthiole*, 1578, preface of Jean des Moulins,
a 4ʳ⁻ᵛ.

C L.
GALENI
DE CRISIBVS
LIBRI TRES,

NICOLAO LEONICENO
INTERPRETE,

Nunc ab omnibus quibus scatebant mendis
repurgati, cum copiosissimo Indice
in hac vltima impressione
adiecto.

REM MAXIMAM SIBI — PROMITTIT PRVDENTIA

LVGDVNI
Apud Gulielmum Rouillium.

M. D. XLVII.

FIGURE 2. The title page of one of the early medical textbooks which Rouillé published. Shows an early publisher's
mark with a motto on "prudence." From the T. G. H. Drake
Collection, Toronto Academy of Medicine.

period always signified Christ's triumph over Satan. Rouillé's eagle, however, stands proudly on the sphere of the world and it is the conditions of worldly triumph that his two mottoes proclaim—prudence, and then *virtus* and *fortuna*.[70]

Some of the time, though, he must have pondered his salvation, and it seems that it was to the Bible that he turned, as Protestants and Erasmian Catholics were doing throughout Europe.[71] Whatever the case, his situation in Lyon in the 1540's and 1550's explains why in those years he published nineteen Bibles and New Testaments, fifteen of them in the vernacular. First, most of his colleagues and partners in the publishing business were near-Protestants or actually attending Protestant conventicles.[72] Secondly, the man who made him his large long-term loan was Hélouin Du Lin, an important Protestant who had earlier financed Etienne Dolet's many evangelical publications.[73] Dolet went to the stake because of them in 1546. Rouillé confined himself to Bibles and was careful to dedicate some of them to the Archbishop of Lyon, whom he called "defender of the Holy Faith."[74]

[70]Rudolf Wittkower, "Eagle and Serpent, A Study in the Migration of Symbols," *Journal of the Warburg Institute*, II (1938–9), 293–325. I am grateful to W. McAllister Johnson for calling this article to my attention. Rouillé's motto changes in 1549.

[71]Rouillé's *Promptuary of Medallions* shows evidence of biblical study in his treatment of religious figures, though he shies away from all doctrinal questions. Like the Bible, the *Promptuary* is divided into two books, part two beginning with the birth of Jesus Christ. The intermingling of pagan deities with Jewish figures, however, reflects a humanist view of pre-Christian antiquity.

[72]This is treated fully in my forth-coming book *Strikes and Salvation at Lyons.*

[73]C. A. Mayer discusses the significance of Du Lin's religious views for Dolet's publications in "The Problem of Dolet's Evangelical Publications," *Bibliothèque d'humanisme et renaissance*, XVII (1955), 405–14.

[74]*Il Nuovo Testamento di Giesu Christo Salvatore Nostro*, 1552, 3–4 (Newberry) "Al l'illustrissimo et reverendissimo Monsignor Cardinal de Tornon, Arcivesco . . . di Lione." The 1547 Italian New Testament was dedicated to Ippolito d'Este, who was then Archbishop. I will take up the character of Rouillé's biblical editions in another place. A few of his editions found their way to an Index, such as a 1545 New Testament in Latin (Reusch, 206).

IL
CORTEGIANO
DEL CONTE BAL-
DESAR CASTI-
GLIONE,

*

*Di nuouo rincontrato con l'originale
scritto di mano de l'auttore:*

Con vna brieue raccolta delle conditioni, che
si ricercano à perfetto Cortegiano, & à
Donna di Palazzo,

IN LYONE APPRES-
so Gulielmo Rouillio.

1550.

FIGURE 3. A later publisher's motto used by Rouillé. From
the collection in the University of Toronto Library.

The turning point for Rouillé was 1560 or 1561. In the autumn of 1560, the Protestants in Lyon staged an armed uprising. It was put down, but the following June there was blood again. A young Huguenot painter threw himself on a Catholic procession and profaned the host. An angry Catholic mob then moved to the Collège de la Trinité and there murdered Rouillé's friend and editor, Barthélemy Aneau.[75] The same year Rouillé published one of his very few polemical editions: Henry VIII's *Assertio* against Luther with a long introduction by a local Catholic leader, the canon-count Gabriel de Saconay. Later in the 1560's, in what he described as an "oblation," the decrees of Trent and the Tridentine Index appeared under his mark as did some serious Catholic works, such as the *Confessio* of the Polish Cardinal Stanislaus Hosius.[76] His political career dates from these years, when the Consulate of Lyon was an impeccably Catholic body and Rouillé had terrible decisions to make concerning his friends and associates in publishing. Instead of the vernacular Bibles which he had once called "the foundation of our faith and salvation," he now offered Bible pictures with vernacular verses. It was a safe genre and one which Lyonese humanists had long approved.[77]

[75]A. Péricaud, "Notes et documents pour servir à l'histoire de Lyon, 1560–1574," *Annuaire de la ville de Lyon et du Département du Rhône* (1842), 2nd part, 4–5, among several sources on this episode. The question of Aneau's "real" religious views, about which G. Brasart-de Groer and Henri Meylan disagree, I will consider in my study of the religion of Rouillé.

[76]*Regis Angliae Henrici Huius Nominis Octavi Assertio Septem Sacramentorum adversus Martinum Lutherum*, 1561 (Pierpont Morgan), iii–lxxxxvi: "Gabriel de Saconay, Ecclesiae Lugdunensis praecentor Pio Lectori." His earliest editions of the Canons of Trent (1564, Houghton, see appendix; 1566, Houghton, Union Theological, Victoria Centre for Reformation and Renaissance Studies) reproduce the Italian editions. His 1572 edition (Newberry) has his own brief preface (A 2^r) and certain new annotations. See Baudrier, IX, 288, 294, 295, 299, 313 for his editions of Hosius, Sonnius, and Saconay.

[77]*Il Nuovo Testamento*, 1552, 4. See n.41 above for editions of the vernacular Bible pictures.

Thus we have some of the reasons behind Guillaume Rouillé's publishing policy. About all of his editions, Rouillé would have said, as publishers always did in the sixteenth century, "I am serving the public."[78] The printers' journeymen had their doubts, claiming that the publishers were men of "immoderate avarice," who wanted 150 per cent profit on their editions;[79] but I think that publishers often believed that they were putting the public's interest above their own time and labour. Rouillé not only trafficked in books; he helped to create them. Also, he had high standards of what a publisher should guarantee about a book. A book should be correct, beautiful, ordered, and convenient.

Every printing shop of any size had at least one journeyman who specialized in correcting. At other times the master printer did the proofreading. Rouillé ordinarily did not rely on artisan labour for this task, however. Sometimes he did the correcting; sometimes he prevailed upon the author.[80] In other cases he found a specialist. For instance, his Spanish edition of the emblems of Giovio and Simeoni, Rouillé gave to a learned Castillian visiting in Lyon, since he himself knew only enough Spanish for business.[81] His edition of Rondelet's *Method of Curing* he turned over to a physician who had been the

---

[78]For instance, in the *Historia Generalis Plantarum,**3ʳ; "semper enim fui, ac etiamnum sum, ita publicae utilitatis appetens, ut in iis obeundis quibus omnium commoda procurentur, nec labori parcam, nec sumptui."

[79]*Remonstrance et Memoires, pour les Compagnons Imprimeurs, de Paris et Lyons: Opposans Contre les Libraires, Maistres Imprimeurs desdits lieux* (n.p. [Lyon], n.d. [1572]), C ii ʳ.

[80]At end of the 1556 Italian edition of Du Choul's *Discorso sopra la Castrametatione,* Rouillé explained that Du Choul and the translator Simeoni had had to leave before the work had been completely set and he hoped that not too many errors had appeared in the work because of their departure. Thus, it is clear that they had been correcting proofs for part of the work.

[81]*Dialogo de las Empresas Militares y Amorosas Compuesto en lengus italiana, Por el illustre y reverendissimo Senor Paulo Iovio . . . Con un Razonamiento . . . del magnifico Senor Ludovico Domeniqui: Todo nuevamente traduzido en Romance Castellano, por Alonso de Ulloa,* 1561, **1ᵛ (Houghton); the learned Castillian was Hernan Perez.

author's friend.[82] Many other publishers followed this same procedure.

Rouillé's ideas about the beauty of a book may have been more unusual. To him beauty was an essential ingredient in the transformation of a work from manuscript to type. For some works publishers see to it that "from one neglected, dirty original emerge many thousands of copies, printed in the most beautiful type."[83] And to an author of a book about emblems he wrote, "you have sent me your manuscript in the most beautiful handwriting and with pictures made by hand; I return it to you printed in the most beautiful type and with the figures all engraved."[84] This beauty of type, ornament, arrangement, and illustration was not easy to achieve. Rouillé was always deciding about his books what Horace had enjoined the poet to decide about his poems: what was appropriate? what was suitable?[85] Rouillé may have experienced this most intensely in connection with his emblem, where plate, motto, and verse had to match perfectly. But to him, finding ornaments appropriate for, say, a sextodecimo edition of Petrarch was just another version of the emblem problem.[86]

The choice of his printers then loomed large for Rouillé, and about his illustrations he fussed even more. Only the best painters and designers would do.[87] The Giovio-Domenichi

[82]*Gulielmi Rondeletii . . . Methodus curandorum omnium morborum*, 2r-3r.

[83]*Elucidatio Paraphrastica in Librum D. Iob . . . Authore F. Fran. Titelmanno Hassellensi*, 1554, 4 (Victoria Centre for Reformation and Renaissance Studies, not in Baudrier).

[84]*Dialogo dell'Imprese Militari et Amorose di Monsignor Giovio . . . Con un Ragionamento de Messer Lodovico Domenichi*, 1559, a 2v, letter to Domenichi.

[85]See Bernard Weinberg's *A History of Literary Criticism in the Italian Renaissance* (Chicago, 1961), 75, 81ff. and many other places. Both Ridolfi (*Ibid.*, 183–4) and Aneau, who wrote *Picta Poesis*, could have discussed the matter of "appropriateness" with Rouillé.

[86]*Il Petrarca*, 1558, 5.

[87]See Baudrier, IX, 42–59 and the excellent discussion of Rouillé's illustrations in Mortimer, *op. cit.* Baudrier feels the beauty of Rouillé's editions was marred by the fast work which he demanded from his *engra-*

Emblems were held up about two years because Rouillé's artists were busy drawing Roman soldiers for Du Choul's *Discourses*.[88] For other editions, Rouillé was to wait through plague and religious persecution till the men he wanted were free to work for him.[89]

Books were to be beautiful, but they were also to be orderly and convenient. Father Ong has suggested to us some important connections between the format of printed books in the sixteenth century and popular Ramist thought, with its stress on the spatial organization of knowledge and easy method for learning.[90] In some ways, Rouillé fits into this development. The good indexes to his books—always announced on the title page; the table of rhymes in Petrarch, with its introduction on its use; the vocabulary of difficult words in the Dante; the summaries of Galen at the beginning and end of every chapter,[91] such aids made it easier and faster to read these books. Furthermore in justifying the organization he had introduced into some of his editions, notably the Alciati emblems and the poems of Marot, he used arguments that Ramus would have approved. "It is very irritating to go looking for a poem when they're not in any order;" "it's much easier to find things when they are each disposed in place and not scattered haphazardly."[92]

---

vers. Yet the verbal evidence suggests that he could be very patient. The Spanish edition of the Alciati's Emblems does show signs of haste, however. It appeared just when Rouillé's output was increasing rapidly.

[88]*Dialogo dell'Imprese*, 1559, a 2ʳ.

[89]*Figures du Nouveau Testament*, 1570, Aa 2 ᵛ–Aa 3ʳ *Commentaires de . . . Matthiole*, 1578, a 4 ʳ–ᵛ. The Protestant designer Pierre Eskrich was probably the main artist Rouillé was waiting for.

[90]Walter J. Ong, S.J., *Ramus, Method, and the Decay of Dialogue* (Cambridge, Mass., 1958), especially 307–18.

[91]*De Morborum et symptomatum differentiis et causis*, 1550, 3–4.

[92]Baudrier, IX, 139; *Emblemata Andrea Alciati*, 1548, 2–3, also reproduced in French in the Preface of Aneau's translation, 1549, 6. Aneau has added his own comments to the end of Rouillé's original preface. Rouillé published one work by Ramus, namely, his *Dialecticarum Libri Tres* (Baudrier, IX, 210).

On the other hand, Rouillé's criteria for classification were not those of the Ramists, even though he used one of their favourite expressions—"common places" or *loci communes*[93]—to describe what he was doing. For instance, to the Alciati emblems he gave, perhaps with Aneau's help, an order which lasted for centuries.[94] It was not based on the Ramist successive dichotomies, nor did it move from the general to the specific. Rather he disposed things according to Horace's rhetorical idea of appropriateness. One moved from the highest, most lofty subjects to the lowest and most earthly. The contrasts that were set up were simple old-fashioned opposites: faith, treachery, courage, cowardice, and the like. And Rouillé went on to say that this added to the book something for which Ramus cared very little, namely beauty. When each thing is in its proper place, the reader's eyes are delighted by beauty.[95] This whole question might well be examined in regard to other publishers who were interested both in organization and in beauty.

To achieve what he did in the range, quantity, and

---

[93]*Emblemata*, 1548. *Loci communes* are stressed in the title, "locorum communium ordine," and in the privilege and the preface. See Ong, chap. 5 and *passim* on the commonplaces. Rouillé's use of the term partakes both of its Ramist meaning, which involves locating and separating things spatially, and its old rhetorical meaning, which involves a collection of phrases or images all " 'common' to any number of cases or occasions for insertion into an oration" (Ong's definition in "Oral Residue in Tudor Prose Style," *PMLA*, LXXX (1965), 150. At least in the case of the emblems, if not in that of Marot's poems, Rouillé's ordering was of images and mottoes that could be used by an orator.

[94]A testimonial to the efficacy of Rouillé's organization is found in the copy of the 1549 Spanish edition of the *Emblems* at the University of Toronto. Though it seems to have come out a few months after Rouillé ordered Latin version of the Emblems, the Spanish edition is not arranged in "loci communes." Perhaps this was due to the opposition of the translator Bernardino Daza. At any rate, the sixteenth-century owner of the Toronto copy has written next to each image the page number of that image in Rouillé's ordered Italian or Latin edition.

[95]*Emblemata*, 1548, 2–3. Cf. Ong, *Ramus*, 91, chap. XII and Weinberg, *Literary Criticism*, 83.

quality of his publications, Rouillé had to maintain good relations with many authors, translators, editors, and designers. Unwilling though he was to cope directly with printers' journeymen, in dealing with literary men and artists he was a master. Not many publishers could have handled so deftly both the Italian Luca Antonio Ridolfi and Barthélemey Aneau, who was denouncing Italians for their "monkeyshines" and the Italian corruption of France.[96] Not many publishers could have managed an edition of Bible pictures in which the Huguenot Pierre Eskrich did the designs and the ardent Catholic Claude de Pontoux the verses.[97] He also knew enough to allow gifted editors a free hand. Whereas in some of his editions, Rouillé's personality is strongly present through letters to the reader and dedications, in the books which Denis Sauvage edited or translated for him, Rouillé hardly says a word. In these books it is Sauvage who explains where the manuscripts have come from and what the system of translating, punctuating, and editing has been.

Furthermore, Rouillé tried never to appear high-handed in editing an author's work. Marot was dead when Rouillé published his poems, yet Rouillé felt he should respect to some extent the order the poet had given to his verses. For the rearrangement of the poems according to verse form, then, Rouillé sought advice from others and especially from a poet who had been Marot's close friend.[98]

What Rouillé paid his editors, translators, and authors, I do not know, though he seems to have sent them books as gifts.[99] He wooed them by dedicating editions to them.[100] He flattered

[96]Chamard, I, 213.

[97]Baudrier, III, 265 for independent evidence of Pontoux' religious views.

[98]Baudrier, IX, 179.

[99]*Ibid.*, 227: Rouillé had sent Poldo d'Albenas a copy of Cardano's treatise on Ptolemy, a work, incidentally, which Rouillé had not published himself.

[100]For instance, the 1552 Dante is dedicated to Ridolfi and Sanchez de las Brozas' *Commentaries on Alciati*, to Navaro.

them by putting their biographies in his *Promptuary of Medallions*. When he felt he had wronged a writer, as in taking so long with the Giovio-Domenichi *Emblems* or in publishing the Spanish version of *Orlando Furioso* without asking the translator's permission, he tried to set the matter straight publicly and in print[101]—surely an unusual act in the sixteenth, if not in any century. But there is no need for me to go on praising Rouillé. Here is what Denis Sauvage said:

Considering the little esteem in which translators, commentators and restorers of corrupt texts are held and the meager reward they get for their labour, I had decided not to do this kind of work, but to remain free for the study which pleased me and could be more properly called my own. But the great honour and fairness with which I saw the Sire Guillaume Rouillé treat literary men and which he showed toward me has broken the firmness of my resolve. At his prayer, I have turned to this work.[102]

When Rouillé died in 1589, the age of the learned printer was over in France. Sébastien Gryphius' son had sold the presses and become a merchant-publisher; Jean de Tournes' son had fled to Geneva. The religious wars and unresolved economic conflict were transforming all French master printers into mere craftsmen. The learned merchant-publisher, however, was a more viable economic type in France, for reasons which are in large part suggested by Rouillé's career. Even then, it was not till the time of the *Encyclopédie* that France again saw publishers of the stature of Guillaume Rouillé.[103]

101*Dialogo dell'Imprese Militari et Amorose*, 1559, a 2^{r-v}. The 1550 Spanish edition of *Orlando Furioso* has no dedication from Rouillé, just a note to the readers. The 1556 edition is dedicated to the translator Urrea. In it he explains the circumstances of the two publications and says he hopes that the 1550 edition had pleased Urrea (α2^{r-v}). Similarly he tried to placate Nicolas de Nicolay for publishing one of his letters without express permission (Baudrier, IX, 38).

102*Philosophie d'Amour de M. Leon Hebreu*, 7.

103See Febvre and Martin, 233–238 on this general decline.

ROUILLÉ EDITIONS NOT KNOWN TO BAUDRIER[1]

Here is a chronological list of twenty-nine editions published by Rouillé which were not found by Jules Baudrier at the time he compiled his bibliography. They are located in North American libraries, the Wellcome Historical Medical Library in London,[2] and in the Library of the University of Aberdeen.[3] I have also added six works which Baudrier knew by name only but for which he had never located a copy. I make no pretence at completeness in this list; there are undoubtedly many more such editions on this continent and in Europe. Where publishers' marks are given, they are numbered according to the numerals assigned by Baudrier, IX, 67–73.

1545

Compendium Naturalis Phylosophiae, seu De consideratione rerum Naturalium earum que ad suum Creatorem reductione, Libri XII: Authore Francisco Titelmanno Hassellensi, ordinis fratrum minorum sanctarum scripturarum apud Louvanienses praelectore (mark 10), Lugduni, Apud Gulielmum Rouilium.
University of Michigan

1546

Clenardi Grammaticae Institutiones Graecae: Eiusdem item sequentia, Annotationes in nominum verborumque difficultates: Investigatio thematis in verbis anomalis cum indice: Compendiosa et exacta Syntaseis ratio (mark 10), Lugduni, Apud Guilielum Rovilium.

[1]Certain of these editions I was unable to see myself. I want to thank the following librarians for providing me with information about them: the Librarian of the Harvard Law School Library; Mrs. Laura B. Hawke of the University of Michigan Medical Center Library; Mr. Wilson G. Duprey of the Prints Division of the New York Public Library and Mr. J. T. Rankin of the Art and Architecture Division of the New York Public Library; Mr. Richard H. Pachella, McAlpin Librarian of the Union Theological Seminary.

[2]*A Catalogue of Printed Books in the Wellcome Historical Medical Library* (London, 1962), I.

[3]W. P. D. Wightman, *Science and the Renaissance: An annotated Bibliography of the Sixteenth-Century Books relating to the Sciences in the Library of the University of Aberdeen* (London, 1962).

At the end, with a new pagination, but no new title page:
Annotationes Renati Guillonii in Grammaticam Graecam Clenardi.

Newberry Library

Clenardi Meditationes Graecae in artem grammaticam: Eae in eorum gratiam qui viva praeceptoris voce destituti sunt (mark 10), Lugduni, Apud Guilielmum Rouilium.

Newberry Library

1549
Fernelius Io . . . De vacuandi ratione liber, quem vulgatiori Nomine Practicam possumus inscribere.

University of Aberdeen, Whitman #250

Tractatus Mysteriorum Missae, cum duplici Canonia expositione Meditationes pro cordis in Deo stabilitatione, Francisci Titelmanni (mark 20), Lugduni, Apud Guillielmum Rouillium.

University of Wisconsin

1550
Fuchs, Leonhard. *Methodus seu ratio compendiaria perveniendi ad culmen medicinae, nunc . . . recognita: Adjuncti de usitate temporis componendorum, miscendorumque medicamentorum ratione libri tres.* Printed by Philibert Rollet for Rouillé.

Wellcome #6883

Horae in Laudem beatissimae virginis Mariae ad vium Romanum. Accesserunt denuo aliquot suffragia. Lugd., Apud Guliel. Rovillium. 168ᵛ Lugduni Mathias Bonhomme excudebat.

Baudrier, IX, 173 by name only
New York Public Library

Il Cortegiano del Conte Baldesar Castiglione, Di nuovo rincontrato con l'originale scritto di mano de l'auttore: con una brieve raccolta delle conditioni, che si recercano à perfetto Cortegiano e à Donna di Palazzo (mark 5). In Lyone, Appresso Gulielmo Rouillio. (See figure, p. 96.)

Baudrier, IX, 174 by name only
University of Michigan——University of Toronto

1551

Testamenti Novi Editio Vulgata. Lugduni Apud Gulielmum Rouillium. Following the Index: Lugduni, Excudebat Philibertus Rolletus.

Union Theological Seminary

Titelmann, Franciscus, *Compendium philosophiae naturalis, seu de consideratione rerum naturalium, earumque ad suum Creatorem reductione: Libri XII.* Printed by Philibert Rollet for Rouillé.
Baudrier, IX, 184, by name only
Wellcome #6309

1553

Enchiridion titulorum aliquot juris, videlicet, de verborum et rerum significatione ex Pandectis; de regulis juris, tum ex Pandectis, tum ex Decretalibus et Sexto; de gradibus affinitatis, ex Pandectis; ad haec rubricae omnes caesarei & pontificii juris. Lugduni, Apud Gulielmum Rouillium, excudebat Philibertus Rolletius.
Harvard Law School

Tractatus de pensionibus ecclesiasticis, Hieronymo Gigante . . . autore: Adiecta est in calce operis tabula quaestionum secundum ordinem quo sunt annotatae. Lugduni, apud Guliel. Rouillium.
Harvard Law School

1554

Elucidatio Paraphrastica in Librum D. Iob, Priore aeditione multò castigatior, adiectis Annotationibus in loca difficiliora, Authore F. Fran. Titelmanno Hassellensi, ordinis Minorum, Accessit recens Index copiosus, cum aliis quibusdam, quae diligens lector animadvertet (mark 6). Lugduni, Apud Gulielmum Rouillium. colophon: Lugduni, Excudebat Ioannes Ausultus. (See figure, p. 109.)

Victoria Centre of Reformation and Renaissance
Studies in the University of Toronto

*Le Nouveau Testament de Nostre Seigneur Iesus Christ, Latin
et Francoys: les deux translations traduictes de Grec, respondantes
L'une à l'autre verset à verset* (title in border). A Lyon, Par
Guillaume Rouille.

Baudrier, IX, 216 by name only
New York Public Library

1555

M. Tul. *Ciceronis Sententiae Insigniores, Apophthegmata Para-
bolae, seu similis, atque eiusdem aliquot piae sententiae. Omnia
Petri Lagnerii Compendiensis opera congesta. Una cum aliorum
aliquot autorum utilissimis sententiis ab eodem Lagnerio collectis:
Quibus accesserunt P. Terentii insigniores sententiae* (mark 8)
Lugduni, Apud Gulielmum Rovillium.
colophon: Lugduni. Excudebat Bartholomaeus Frein.

Newberry Library

1556

*Epistre consolatoire de Messire Iean Boccace, envoyee au Signeur
Pino de Rossi Traduicte d'Italien en Françoys par Damoiselle
Marguerite de Cambis, Baronne d'Aigremont et Lieutenante de
Nismes.* A Lyon, Par Guillaume Roville.

Baudrier IX, 230 by name only
Houghton Library

1557

Hieronymi Cardani Mediolanensis Medici Liber de Libris Propriis
(mark 1). Apud Gulielmum Rovillium.
Houghton Library   Newberry Library   Wellcome #1301

M. Tul. *Ciceronis Sententiae insignories, Apophthegmata, Para-
bolae, seu Similia, atque eiusdem aliquot piae sententiae: Quibus
alias* [two words erased and "alleture damnato" written by hand]

aliquot sutoribus, ut Terentio, Erasmo, sed praecipuè ex Apoph-thegmatum libris, et aliis, quam utilissimas adiecimus: Omnia Petri Lagnerii Compendiensis opera collecta, et congesta (mark 6) Lugduni, Apud Gulielmum Rouuillium. Copy owned by a Spaniard in 1633.

Houghton Library

1559

Le imprese heroiche et morali ritrovate da M. Gabriello Symeoni Fiorentino, al Gran Conestabile de Francia (mark 16). In Lyone, Appresso Guglielmo Rovillio.

Baudrier, IX, 260 by name only
Newberry Library

1560

Tagault, Jean. *De chirurgica institutione libri quinque. His accessit sextus liber de materia chirurgica, authore Iacobe Hollerio Stempano.*

Wellcome #6206

1562

Petri Gylli De Bosopore Thracio Libri III (mark 16). Lugduni, Apud Gulielmum Rovillium. Probably a reissue of the 1561 edition.

Houghton Library

Practica causarum criminallium D. Ludovici Carerii Rheginensis . . . tyronibus ac veteranis admodùm utilis & necessaria, in quo Tractatus appellationum, Tract. de indiciis & tortura, Tract. de homicidio & de haereticis continentur, & quae disponantur super his iure civili, cano. & Regni neap. statutis traduntur, & miro ordine apparent, compilata, postrema hac editione ab autore ipso diligentissimè recognita, & tertia ampliùs parte locupletata, cum iiusdem autoris summariis & copiosissimo indice. Lugduni, apud G. Rovillium.

Harvard Law School

ELVCIDA

TIO PARAPHRA-
STICA IN LI-
BRVM D. IOB,

Priore æditione multò caſtigatior,
adiectis Annotationibus in
loca difficiliora,

AVTHORE F. FRAN. TITEL-
manno Haſſellenſi,ordinis Minorum.

Acceſsit recèns Index copioſus, cu.n alijs
quibuſdam,quæ diligens le-
ctor animaduertet.

IN VIRTVTE

ET FORTVNA.

L V G D V N I,

Apud Gulielmum Rouillium.

M. D. LIIII.

Tiraqueau, André. . . . *In tit. res inter alios actas aliis non praeiu-
dicare commentarij: Eiusdem in titul. de iudicio in rebus exiguis
ferendo tractatus: Nunc primùm in lucem editus* . . . Lugduni,
apud Guliel. Rovillium.

Harvard Law School

1564

*Canones, et Decreta Sacrosancti œcumenici et Generalis Concilii
Tridenti, Sub Paulo III, Iulio III, Pio IIII, Pontificibus Max.*: *Cum
prototypis et originalibus à Secretario et Notariis dicti Concilii
collati, qui in operis fine subscripserunt, summa fide et diligentia
nunc postremò excusi* (mark 16). Lugduni, Apud Guliel. Rovillium. Not the same as the edition listed in Baudrier, IX, 293.
Copy belonging to Cardinal de Lorraine.

Houghton Library

*Index Librorum Prohibitorum, Cum Regulis confectis per Patres
a Tridentina Synodo delectos, auctoritate Sanctisa: D. N. Pii IIII
Pont. Max. comprobatos* (mark 16). Lugduni, Apud Guliel.
Rovillium. Bound with the above; copy of the Cardinal de
Lorraine.

Houghton Library

*Horatius: M. Antonii Mureti in Eundem Annotationes, Aldi
Manuti de metris Horationes, Eiusdem Annotationes in Horatium*
(mark 4) Lugduni, Apud Guliel. Rovillium.
Colophon: Lugduni apud Philibertum Rolletum. A reissue of an
earlier edition, as Rollet was dead by 1564.

Columbia University

1565

Cardano, Girolamo . . . *de Methodo Medendi sectiones quatuor*
Paris, G. Rovillius MDXLV for 1565, at which period Rouillé
published a few editions in Paris with his nephew.

University of Aberdeen, Whitman #132

1566

Kling, Melchior: *In Quatuor institutionum iuris principis Iustiniani libros enarrationes.* . . . *Priori aeditioni, praeter quàm quòd à multis est repurgata mendis.* . . . *Cum indice locupletissimo* Lugduni, apud Guliel. Rovillium.

Harvard Law School

1569

Orlando Furioso di M. Lodovico Ariosto, Revisto et Ristampato sopra le correttioni de Ieronimo Ruscelli: Con l'aggiunta de i cinque canti nuovi, Insieme gli Argomenti, Allegorie & espositione de i vocaboli difficili, Et una Tavola generale di tutte le materie principali contenute nel libro (mark 8). In Lyone, Appresso Gugliel. Rovillio.

Houghton Library

1575

Rondelet, Guillaume: *Methodus curandorum omnium morborum corporis humani in tres libros distincta.*

Wellcome #5554

1576

Amati Lusitani . . . *Curationum medicinalium, Centuriae Duae, Quinta et Sexta.*

University of Aberdeen, Whitman #32g

1576

Rondelet, Guillaume: *Methodus curandorum omnium morborum corporis humani in tres libros distincta.*

University of Aberdeen, Whitman #581

1579

Loci argumentorum legales, d. Nicolao Everardo . . . *auctore: Nunc recèns recogniti, emendati, summarijs illustrati, ac P. Prateij adnotatiunculis locupletati* Lugduni, apud Gulielmum Rouillium.

Harvard Law School

Guillaume Rouillé

1589

Pauli Aeginetae Medici Opera, Ioanne Guinterio Andernaco Medico peritissimo Interprete: Eiusdem Guinterij, & Iani Cornarij Annotationes: Item, Iacobi Goupyli, & Iacobi Dalechampij Scholia in eadem opera; Cum indice copiosissimo, ac locupletissimo (mark 4). Lugduni, Apud Gulielmum Rovillium.

University of Michigan Medical Center Library
Wellcome #4873

Practica causarum criminalium in. Ludovici Carerii . . . Tyronibus, ac veteranis admodùm utilis, & necessaria, in qua appellationum, indiciorum & torturae, homicidij, & assassinij, & haeresis tractatus continentur, & quae disponantur super his iure civili, canon. & regni Neapol. statutis traduntur, & miro ordine apparent compilata: Postrema hac editione ab auctore ipso diligentissimè recognita, & tertia ampliùs parte locupletata Lugduni, apud Gulielmum Rovillium.

Harvard Law School

GERMAN
ZEITUNG LITERATURE
IN THE SIXTEENTH CENTURY

Max Kortepeter*

HE ANGLO-SAXON verb *tīdan* meaning "to take place, happen, occur" gave rise to the English word "tiding" and is cognate with the German word *Zeitung*.[1] Essentially *Zeitung*, at the beginning of the sixteenth century, still referred to oral or written "tidings" but by the close of the century, the word had already begun to take on its modern denotation of "newspaper," that is, tidings characterized by their regular appearance in print. Of course, this transformation is intimately connected with the invention and the spread of the printing press. Such a transformation also provides ample evidence, in the vein of McLuhan's theses, of important changes wrought in the social structure of the age by the use of the printing press in sixteenth-century society.[2] But the use and development of the

*I should like to acknowledge the encouragement and help given to me by Mr. V. J. Parry, lecturer in Middle East history at the School of Oriental and African Studies, London University, who first called my attention to the importance of *Zeitung* literature for the study of East European history.

[1] F. Kluge, *Etymologisches Wörterbuch der Deutschen Sprache* (Berlin, 1960), 881: "Zeitung."

[2] M. McLuhan, *The Gutenberg Galaxy* (Toronto, 1965), 1–5.

Zeitung in the sixteenth century paved the way not only for the modern newspaper, it equally gave rise to a particular genre of historiography which also appeared toward the end of the same century. In fact, the *Zeitungen* and other closely related materials such as the *relationes*, although as yet inadequately explored, have long been recognized as constituting a valuable source for the social, economic, and political history of the sixteenth century. I should like to review what I consider to be the most important events in the development of *zeitung* literature during the century of the Reformation. As the events unfold, we shall catch vivid glimpses of the manner in which the structure of mediaeval society was transformed by the press. Moreover, in the course of sketching-in this background, I hope to provide a few observations on the difficulties confronting a historian who wishes to make use of the *Zeitungen* or the historiography based upon them.

The ultimate source of news in the sixteenth century was the spectacular events themselves. The world was then experiencing an upheaval which compares favorably with that of the present century. Among the earliest of "tidings" disseminated throughout Europe either in the form of letters, fly sheets, or broad sheets (known in Germany as *Flugschriften* and *Einblattdruck*) was the description by Christopher Columbus of his discoveries in the New World. Shortly thereafter news of the startling advances of the Ottoman Turks against Christianity, both on land and sea, came to occupy the alarmed attention of the entire Continent. Egypt and Algiers fell to the Sultan in 1517. Against the background of the breakdown of the Hungarian monarchy, the capitulation of Belgrade in 1521 and the Battle of Mohács in 1526 virtually marked the end of Hungarian resistance. Three years later the Janissaries were at the gates of Vienna and by 1536, Sultan Suleiman and Francis I of France had concluded a solemn alliance which shocked Europe but which generally served to protect both France and the Ottomans from the Spanish and Austrian Habsburgs for the succeeding three centuries.[3] On the Mediterranean, except for the interlude of Lepanto, the Ottomans held Spain at bay and gradually reduced Venice to neutrality. It is no wonder then that the countless *Zeitungen* of the so-called *Türkengefahr* (Threat of the Turks) kept press and pen active throughout the century. The high interest and actual risks for Western Europe also account for the availability of not a few "tidings" about the more remote, but highly significant wars between the Ottoman Turks and the Safavid Persians. In Eastern Europe, even the smallest successes of Cossack raids upon Ottoman towns were heralded with *Zeitungen* in five languages.

Coinciding with the collapse of Mamluk Egypt, Germany became very prominent in the news reports after 1517 following the appearance of Luther's "95 theses." Indeed, for the next hundred years "tidings" of the progress of the Reformation vied with the *Türkengefahr* for favorite billing in every print shop, book stall, and country fair throughout Europe.[4] The chief contestants in these grandiose struggles became national and international heroes and, in fact, the medium of the *Zeitung* was adopted rapidly by all contenders during the Wars of Religion and, unilaterally, by the Europeans at

[3]The standard study of the *Zeitung* literature has been prepared by the tireless bibliographer, Karl Schottenloher, *Flugblatt und Zeitung* (*Bibliothek für Kunst- und Antiquitätssammler* Bd. 21: Berlin, 1922). Typical of the "Neue Zeitung" appearing at the time of the siege of Vienna was one entitled ". . . The siege of the city of Vienna in Austria by the most terrible tyrant and destroyer of Christianity, the Turkish Emperor, known as Sultan Suleiman . . ." (*ibid.*, 168). One may consult D. M. Vaughan, *Europe and the Turk, a Pattern of Alliances* (Liverpool, 1954) for details about the French-Ottoman treaty. Cf. also J. Kirchner, *Das deutsche Zeitschriftenwesen: Seine Geschichte und seine Probleme*, I (Leipzig, 1942) (not seen).

[4]Students of sixteenth-century history are only now turning to the serious study of the interrelationships of these two great challenges to the old order: the Protestant Reformation and the advance of the Ottoman Turks in Eastern Europe. See for example, Stephen Fischer-Galati, *Ottoman Imperialism and German Protestantism 1521–1555* (Harvard Hist. Monog., 43: Cambridge, 1959).

the time of the Turkish Wars as a dry, and somewhat less than impartial, instrument for imparting general news. Martin Luther, Charles V, Phillip II, Suleiman the Magnificent, the Tatar Khan, Tahmasp, the Shah of Persia, all figure prominently in the reports and each was hated, feared, revered and cursed, depending on the origin of the *Zeitung*, and each frequently was reported as dead. Certain types of *Zeitungen* praised or blamed individual commanders, and described their victories or defeats, while others, known as *Flugschriften*, consisted of religious tracts, sermons, admonitions, and words of comfort. A commander who had lost a battle could, for a small subsidy to a printer, become a national hero. Hence, both the *Zeitung* and the *Flugschrift* were used often to mold public opinion in a manner reminiscent of a similar use made of the troubadours and minnesänger. Among the chief western European events reported in the *Zeitungen* were the composition and developments at the Diet of Worms in 1521, the Peasants' War in 1424–25, the Habsburg Wars with France, the attempts by Emperor Charles V to suppress the Protestant heresies up to the Peace of Augsburg of 1555, the progress and results of the Great Council of Trent, the successes of the Catholic and Protestant parties in France and England, and the attempts by Spain to suppress the rebellion of her Netherlands dependencies.

As the events and the chief contenders of this sixteenth-century drama are lined up in their proper places, one may then begin to search out and evaluate the various centres which developed in Western Europe for the dissemination of news. If, as was doubtless the case, news of Columbus and of the great discoveries passed rapidly to the capitals of Europe largely from Spain, it is equally true that for some years after the turn of the century, the great emporium of news, particularly news of the Mediterranean and of the so-called *Türkengefahr* was Venice. It is true that the Ottoman Turks gradually eliminated the Venetian colonial empire in the eastern Mediterranean, delivering the final blow with the taking of Cyprus in 1570, but in many respects, the Venetian contacts with the Ottoman state remained the best in Europe for another century. Thus the Rialto district of Venice remained one of the primary points in Western Europe for the dissemination of reliable news about the Mediterranean and the Ottoman Empire for the entire century. One need only turn to the British *Calendar of State Papers* pertaining to Venice, the collection of *Le Relazioni degli Ambasciatori Veneti al Senato*, the numerous *Thesori Politichi*, and the important *Négociations de la France dans le Levant* to gain some idea of the vast amount of systemic documentation available to the leading chanceries of Europe in the sixteenth century.[5] The raw material coming into this strategically situated Republic doubtless provided much of the "copy" upon which the daily Rialto bulletins, the *notizie scritte* were based. On the Rialto, one could purchase a page or two of the latest news for the cost of about one Venetian *gazzetta*, hence, the probable origin of our word "gazette." It was no accident that Shakespeare had Salanio, in *The Merchant of Venice* (III, i), ask, "Now, what news on the Rialto?"[6]

While Venice still remained an important centre for the dissemination of news from the Mediterranean and points beyond, the prosperous South German cities of Augsburg and Nürnberg gradually assumed a dominant rôle in the collection and distribution of political and economic "tidings"

[5]E. Alberi edited the *Relazioni* in three series (Florence, 1839–1863) and E. Charrière prepared the *Négociations* in four vols. (Paris, 1848–1860). Cf. also an early study of the history of journalism in Germany which may only be used with caution: L. Salomon, *Geschichte des Deutschen Zeitungswesen*, 2 vols. (Leipzig, 1906), especially 1–34.

[6]The *notizie* apparently first appeared in 1536 during the Venetian War with the Ottoman Turks, see the article "Giornale," *Enciclopedia Italiana*, XVII, 184–185. For notes on the etymology of "gazzetta" see C. Battisti and G. Alessio, *Dizionario Etimologico Italiano*, III (Florence, 1952), 1777: "gazzetta."

especially those deriving from the wide connections of the famed banking house of Fugger. As bankers for both the Pope and the Emperor Charles V, their sources of news concerning the inner workings of the Habsburg Empire were frequently very good indeed. Associated with the House of Fugger was a characteristic series of *Zeitungen* popularly known to us as the "Fugger Newsletters." These largely handwritten newssheets, which in fact were called "nouvellen" by their two principal compilers, Jeremias Crasser and Jeremias Schiffle, were prepared at regular intervals and sent to influential subscribers, chiefly Catholic merchants, clergymen, princes, and rulers.[7] Only when the financial centre of Europe shifted to Antwerp at mid-century did the economic significance of Augsburg and Nürnberg become somewhat diminished. From these centres the financing of the Wars of Religion had been arranged. The Fuggers had advanced enormous sums to Charles V, in 1520, so that he might be elected Emperor, and later they provided the funds for him to prosecute wars against France, the Ottoman Empire, and the Protestant princes. When these undertakings largely failed, Fugger bankruptcy became inevitable and Southern Germany no longer enjoyed a near monopoly in the realm of international finance.[8] Here again it must be noted, however, that the "Fugger *Zeitungen*" or, better, *Nouvellen* continued to be sent to a select number of subscribers to the end of the century and were circulated even more widely through copies made by the various masters of the post (*Postmeister*). The sixteenth

[7]See the excellent discussion of the Fugger Newsletters and their relationship with the *notizie scritte* in Victor von Klarwill, ed. *The Fugger News-Letters* (London, 1924), xiv and *passim*. Von Klarwill in the same place clears up the difference between the "Ordinary" and "Extraordinary Papers." For a more recent critique of the Fugger newsletters, see the article by M. A. H. Fitzler, "Die Entstehung der sogenannten Fuggerzeitungen in der Wiener Nationalbibliothek," *Veröffentlichungen des Wiener Hofkammerarchivs*, II (Vienna, 1937), 1–81.

[8]For the essential economic and financial background of the sixteenth century, consult R. Ehrenberg, *Capital and Finance in the Age of the Renaissance* (New York, 1963; orig. ed., 1928) especially 86–132.

century not only was the century *par excellence* for pamphlets and newsletters, it was also the era marking the rise of post routes to carry the added volume of correspondence. Furthermore, the wide dissemination of political tracts in print also prompted state and church to give considerable attention to problems of censorship in the middle decades of the century.[9]

Upon the outbreak of the Wars of Religion, the Protestant cause derived much of its moral fortitude from the prolific pens of Martin Luther and Melancthon. It is therefore not surprising that a good deal of the Protestant "tidings" as well as religious tracts in the third and fourth decades of the century were prepared in Wittenberg. In fact, the *Zeitungen* in general, for the period spanning the religious wars, have received most of the attention heretofore given to this genre.[10]

By mid-century social and cultural conditions in Germany were such that still another centre for the dissemination of *Zeitungen* and other printed matter developed rapidly. This was the renowned city of Frankfurt am Main. This *Reichsstadt* or "free city" had long been the centre for a number of newsworthy historical events. Soon after the establishment of the printers' trade in the neighboring city of Mainz, Frankfurt began to occupy a special prominence in the German booktrade partly because of the number of printers in the city, partly because of the number of trade routes passing through the city from the four corners of the German Empire.

[9]Cf. Salomon, 31–34; Schottenloher, 207 ff. and the articles by W. Brückner, "Der kaiserliche Bücherkommissar Valentin Leucht" and "Eine Messbuchhändlerliste von 1579 und Beiträge zur Geschichte der Bücherkommission" in *Archiv für Geschichte des Buchwesens*, III, cols. 97–179 and 1629–47.

[10]Cf. for example, the collections noted by P. Hohenemser, *Flugschriftensammlung Gustav Freitag* (Frankfurt a/M, 1925) and by K. M. Kertbény, *Ungarn betreffende deutsche Erstling's-Drucke, 1454–1600* in the series *Bibliografie der ungarischen nationalen und internationalen Literatur*, I (Budapest, 1880), 17–758. C. Göllner, *Turcica; die europäischen Türkendrucke des xvi. jahrhunderts* (Bucharest, 1961), an important study dealing with the reports from the Ottoman realm.

Moreover, at the close of the Schmalkaldic Wars, Frankfurt was situated at a middle point between the major religious blocks and presumably could sell books to both.[11] Vienna and Breslau provided news of Poland, Hungary and points beyond. (The Viennese printers actually took a hand in disseminating their own *Neue Zeitung* toward the end of the century during the thirteen-year Habsburg-Ottoman conflict of 1593–1606.) From Strassburg came news of Switzerland, France, and Spain, while Cologne quickly learned of new developments in England and the Low Countries. The latest "tidings" from Scandinavia and Muscovy could reach the Frankfurt emporium by way of the Hanseatic cities of Lübeck and Hamburg.[12]

A number of eye-witness accounts of the Frankfurt Fair, the origins of which go back at least to the thirteenth century, are available to us but perhaps none is so well-known or so pompous as that composed by Henri Estienne the younger, a scion of the famous French publishing house:

> For even if this "Attic Fair" offered nothing else than houses packed with books of every sort . . . and did not at all add this advantage, that one may there enjoy the discourses and conversations of many learned men, even so, I say, ought not the Fair to be of inestimable value to the followers of the Muses? Indeed, it can provide one with a library hardly less rich . . . than were those libraries, so celebrated in the past, of Ptolemy, of Polycrates, of Pisistratus, and of other princes, and all in such a way as not to force one to go to a regal, that is, to an immense, or rather . . . a monstrous expense.
>
> While Germany thus gathers in that city so great an abundance of books for those interested in literature and the liberal arts, she adds a new service to the old. . . . I speak of that service by which he who invented the art of printing was unwilling to cherish that invention in his own bosom, but shared it with all the world to the highest good of the human race; For one and

[11]An important historical sketch of German printing and of the German booktrade appears in the introduction to James Westfall Thompson's edition of *The Frankfort Book Fair, The Francofordiense Emporium of Henri Estienne* (Chicago, 1911), especially 3–99.

[12]Salomon, *loc. cit.*

the same act shattered and dispelled the dense shades of ignorance; struck from its throne and drove afar that barbarism which had so long reigned everywhere; brought back the exiled Muses, and gave to literature its greatest impulse and its strongest support. As a result of this great service it is no wonder that this country secures such favor from the Muses. And in return, the country shows that it favors the Muses, in other matters, but especially in this very Fair, and that it attends them with an unusual degree of honor. For while the Muses are usually not even admitted to fairs elsewhere, we see them not only admitted to this one, but even received most magnificently, and this in spite of the fact that this Fair is such that, in comparison with others it may be called . . . a veritable workshop of war.

For certain other contemporary observers of the Frankfurt Fair the praise was not always so unqualified. It was Luther who called Frankfurt . . . "that silver and gold hole through which (passes) from German hands everything that flows, grows or is coined and beaten." More to the point, J. W. Thompson, the editor of the exquisite edition and translation of Estienne's *Frankofordiense Emporium*, further drew attention to the street of the booksellers and publishers, the Buchgasse . . . "outside of whose shops were hawked *Flugschriften* and *Zeitungen*."[13]

To recapitulate, by the mid-sixteenth century a number of important centres, each with its own characteristic strong and weak points, were disseminating *Zeitung*-type news reports. Notable among many such European centres were Venice, Augsburg, Nürnberg, Wittenberg, and Frankfurt-am-Main.[14]

[13]Thompson, 173 and 175, 55 and 80, respectively. Cf. also P. Rath, *Das Mess-Memorial des Frankfurter Buchhändlers M. Horder 1569 und der Frankfurter Volksbücherverlag des H. Gülfferich* (Frankfurt, 1926) (not seen) and G. Richter, "Die Sammlung von Drucker-, Verleger- und Buchführer-Katalogen in den Akten der Kaiserlichen Bücherkommission" in *Festschrift für Josef Benzing* (Wiesbaden, 1964), 317–72.

[14]Jean-Pierre Seguin has recently produced a study of *Zeitung* literature in France entitled *L'Information en France de Louis XII à Henry II* (Geneva, 1961) in the series *Travaux d'Humanisme et Renaissance*, XLIV. Another work in the same series is also of interest for this subject: H. Meylen et al, *Aspects de la Propaganda Religieuse* (*Travaux*, XXVIII: Geneva, 1957).

Later in the century Cologne and Vienna were to share this prominence. The *Zeitungen* or "tidings" in the early sixteenth century were chiefly passed from person to person either by word of mouth or through handwritten correspondence. Occasionally a gentleman of means would have had certain news items printed up on a *Flugblatt* or fly sheet to be enclosed with his regular correspondence. The Fugger *Neuvellen* seem also to have been mainly handwritten. During the period of the most active religious polemics, between 1520 and 1555, a number of more dogmatic statements, *Warnung, Instruction,* and theological positions were printed in the form of *Flugschriften.* It would appear that the distinction between the *Zeitung* and the *Flugschrift*, particularly in this period, was sometimes difficult to make if both happened to be printed. Generally speaking, the one purported to be a straightforward, dry relation of events; the other clearly advocated a point of view. These activities were profitable and naturally therefore attracted many imitators and interlopers. Masters of the post often made copies and sold them to the local citizens, and printers in one area hastened to reprint the *Neue Zeitungen* and *Flugschriften* coming their way from other areas. Even the Fugger newsletters clearly contain copies of currently available *Zeitungen* and *Flugschriften*, as do the sixteenth-century document collections previously mentioned.

To my knowledge, no one has yet hazarded a more comprehensive reason, apart from the political events of the time, for the great glut of pamphlet-type printed matter in the middle decades of the sixteenth century. In my opinion this problem is closely related to general overcrowding in the European printing trade during this era. At the time, journeyman printers were wandering as far afield as Mt. Athos, Moldavia, and Muscovy; moreover, except for certain fine editions prepared in Augsburg, Nürnberg, and Lyon, the

[15]Cf. Thompson, 15, citing Dziatzko Art. "Buchhandel" in *Handwörterbuch der Staatswissenschaften*, II, 1128. A number of printers' strikes

printing trade witnessed a distinct retrogression in technique and composition in the first half of the century.[15] Whatever may be the truth of such speculations, we may safely conclude that by 1550 two elements of the modern newspaper existed side by side but they were not, as yet, fused together. Periodicity or near periodicity appears to have been characteristic of the handwritten Fugger *Nouvellen* while more and more frequently the *Zeitungen* were being printed rather than hand written.

In spite of the international pre-eminence of Frankfurt in publishing and printing in the second half of the sixteenth century, as so often happens to those working too closely to their medium, she was robbed of the distinction of developing the *Zeitung* techniques to their next stage. In the city of Cologne about the year 1581, a certain well-born gentleman by the name of Michael von Aitzing, whose family had long held the position of *Hofdiener* (Imperial Servitor) to the Habsburg emperors, brought out the first of a series of what came to be known as *Messrelationen* or "Fair News Sheets" soon to become the characteristic form of *Zeitung* literature in Frankfurt. Von Aitzing, who had studied in the Netherlands, first gained fame for his *Leo Belgicus*, a history of the rebellion of the Netherlands against Spanish rule between the years 1559 and 1581. His next venture into this field, which might be termed "historical *Zeitung*-writing," came in 1583 when he published the *Relatio Historica* dealing with the Catholic-Protestant struggle for the control of the Archbishopric of Cologne. Both of these undertakings proved so successful that in the year 1588, Von Aitzing began bringing out a *Relatio Historica* at half-yearly intervals in which he

which took place during that period bear witness also to the low wages. The reported decline in technique doubtless did not take into consideration the artistic contributions to various *Zeitungen* by famous engravers such as Albrecht Dürer and by such poets as Hans Sachs. Cf. also, H. A. Innis, *Empire and Communications* (Oxford, 1950), 178.

included news from all over Europe. This type of *Zeitung* received the appellation *Messrelationen* for it was turned out each fall and spring to correspond with the opening of the Frankfurt fair. Such a successful venture attracted many imitators even before the death of Von Aitzing in 1593. Unfortunately his successors in compiling *Messrelationen* henceforth tended to be less objective in their selection of material and some used their works to forward one religious viewpoint only. Soon also the *Messrelationen*, from whatever source, were being collected into five-yearly accounts such as the *Relatio Historica Quinquennalis . . . von Anno 1590 bis 1595* (Frankfurt a/m, 1596) compiled by a Lutheran clergyman in Frankfurt who was known by the pseudonym of Jacobus Frankus [Lautenbach]. His chief imitator and successor, T. Meurerius, continued the *Relatio Historica* into the seventeenth century and thus provided Richard Knolles with the concluding events of his *Historie of the Turks* which was printed in London in 1603.[16]

Between the appearance of the first printed "Neue Zeitung" at the turn of the sixteenth century and the appearance of the crude but important *Zeitung* "history" of Jacobus Frankus in 1596 lay almost a century of development in this genre. Thereafter it was a very simple transition indeed, to the full-blown histories appearing in subsequent decades and drawing

[16]For details on Von Aitzing, one must consult F. Stieve, "Ueber die ältesten halbjährigen Zeitungen oder Messrelationen und besonders über deren Begründer Freiherr Michael von Aitzing," *Abhandlung der hist. Classe der Königl. Bayer. Akad. der Wissenschaften*, XVI (Munich, 1883), 177–82 and J. Benzing, "Der Zeitungschreiber Michael von Aitzing und der braunschweigische Hof," *Archiv für Geschichte des Buchwesens*, III, cols. 1621–1626. One might note in passing that the Latin word *Relatio* meant among other things a "report" prepared for the Roman Emperor by his State Secretary. See "Relatio" in the Zeller *Grosses Vollständiges Universal Lexikon*, XXXI (reprint of 1742 ed.; Gratz, 1961), col. 423. The writer would further acknowledge his debt to V. J. Parry for pointing out the use made by Knolles of Meurerius. Mr. Parry is preparing an edition of Knolles. R. Grasshoff in his Inaugural Dissertation at Leipzig University, entitled *Die briefliche Zeitung des XVI Jhdts.* (Leipzig, 1877) noted the close relationship of *Zeitungen* to historiography.

heavily upon the *Zeitung* and *Flugschrift* literature of an entire century to fill out the details of their narratives. If one mentions only one representative printed chronicle from each of the major countries of Western Europe, one is made in some measure aware of the tremendous importance of the *Zeitungen* and of the equally enormous task one faces in attempting to track down the sources of any given chronicle. Ortelius of Nürnberg, whose history of the Turkish wars appeared in 1602, had direct access to *Zeitung* sources through his brother-in-law, the famous copper plate engraver, Johannes Sibmacher.[17] Nicolas Istvanfi composed his history, *De Rebus Ungaricus* after serving as a diplomat and negotiator in the Hungarian Wars.[18] A history of the same sort in Italian, the *Istoria del mondo* (1570–1596), of Cesare Campana drew heavily upon the *relationes* literature and was published in Venice in 1599.[19] A work of similar scope and sources was prepared in France by Nicolas de Montreux.[20] In Austria, Khevenhüller, the biographer of Ferdinand II, drew much of his information on Germany from the *Zeitungen* readily at hand.[21] Yet many of the above-mentioned historians and chroniclers make no mention of their debt to the *Zeitung*

[17]*Chronologia oder Historische Beschreibung aller Kriegsemporungen und Belagerungen . . . so in Ober und Under Ungarn auch Sibenbürgen mit dem Türcken von Ao. 1395 biss auff gegenwertige Zeitt* (Nürnberg, 1602), (2nd. ed. Nürnberg, 1620–22, and a Dutch ed. Amsterdam, 1619). Cf. "Ortelius," *Allgemeine Deutsche Biographie*, XXIV (Leipzig, 1887), 445–6.

[18]*Historiarum de rebus Hungaricis libri XXXIV ab anno 1490 quò Mathias Corvinus rex Hung. fato functus est, ad Mathiam usque*, II (Cologne, 1622). Cf. "Isthvanfius" *Biographie Universelle*, XXI (Paris, 1818), 302.

[19]*Istoria del mondo descritte dal Signor Cesare Campana* (Venice, 1599). According to the article "Campana" in the *Enciclopedia Italiana*, VIII (Milan, 1930), 566, the work was widely acclaimed in its time and a second edition appeared in 1607.

[20]*Histoire universelle des guerres du Turc* (Paris, 1607). For further details see the article "Montreux, Nicolas de," *Grand Dictionnaire universel du XIXᵉ siècle*, XI, 529.

[21]*Annales Ferdinandei* vols. I–IX (Vienna, 1640–46). This work was published posthumously but the entire 12 vols. were not published until the eighteenth century. Cf. "Khevenhüller" (Graf Franz Christoph), *Der Grosse Brockhaus*, X (Leipzig, 1931), 116–17.

literature. Richard Knolles (d. 1610), the Oxford graduate and schoolmaster from Sandwich in Kent, who brought out his famous *Generall Historie of the Turkes from the first beginning of that Nation,* in 1603, is one exception. In his introduction, Knolles refers to the *Zeitungen* in the following manner:

But these [other historians] in the course of so long an history failing also (as by conferring that which is hereafter written, together with their histories, is easily to be perceived) to perfect that I had taken in hand I tooke my refuge unto the writings of such other learned and credible authors, as of whose integritie and faithfulnesse the world hath not to my knowledge at any time yet doubted: yea for these few late years I was glad out of *the German and Italian writers* in their own language in part to borrow the knowledge of these late affaires. . . .[22]

I should like to conclude with a few general remarks about problems of editing as viewed by a student of sixteenth-century Islamic history. Once the proper texts have been located, problems of paleography are likely to consume a large part of the time of an editor or historian working on manuscripts written in the Arabic script. The very nature of the script itself provides endless opportunities for error. For example, the mere misplacing of a dot can change one letter into any of a half-dozen other letters. Apparent synonyms, which in fact may be different words drawn from any one of the three basic languages, Arabic, Persian, or Turkish, as well as the languages of subject minorities present formidable problems. The errors of illiterate (or semi-literate) copyists also multiply the difficulties. The student of toponomy may have difficulties with even such elementary problems as the names of prominent features of the terrain such as rivers, towns, and mountain passes.

[22]Knolles, A3 iii ʳ and ᵛ. Knolles' work was revised and published many times: 1610, 1621, 1638 etc. Cf. "Knolles, Richard," *Dictionary of National Biography*, XXXI (London, 1887), 237–38.

If we turn for a moment to printed texts of sixteenth-century works, a number of problems arise from the use of poor paper, inferior inks and presses, and the usual errors of the compositors. The dearth of critical editions or even of popular editions and translations calls attention both to the shortage of editing skills and the enormous problems involved. Some areas of Islamic studies are hampered greatly for the lack of good dictionaries. Up to the present day, most scholars originating from Islamic countries, while admittedly better equipped linguistically to deal with the Islamic sources than many of their Western European or North American counterparts, still elect to dispute historical problems on the basis of often extremely faulty editions rather than to foster the systematization of archives or to bring out adequate editions of manuscripts or old editions. Admittedly these conditions are fostered as much by grant-giving foundations in the Western World as by the lack of funds in the Middle East. Foundations fortunately are beginning to realize that sound literary and historical work "pays off" often as much as do the so-called "strategic studies." In fact, the one is not possible without the other.

One final point appears to be worth mentioning. In pre-modern Islamic society the Arabic script was looked upon as "Holy Writ" and therefore not to be tampered with by editors or anyone else. During World War I a German officer who could master the Arabic script enough to scribble an unintelligible "message" on a scrap of paper could often get past an illiterate Turkish guard for the same reason. Today in certain Islamic countries the tables are sometimes completely turned. The Arabic script may be looked upon as the instrument of a decadent past. This may account, on occasion, for the ease with which a modern editor discards or changes a word of relevance to a difficult text.

As if these problems were not formidable enough, the historian of the Islamic world is also drawn to contemporaneous sources in West European languages. One might reasonably ask why? Perhaps the most fundamental reason, apart from the desire to expand or corroborate facts, is that often the Islamic chronicles and documents available to us are lacking in descriptive details which are the life-blood of modern historiography.

One final example will suffice to demonstrate the usefulness of what I have termed *"Zeitung* literature." While preparing a historical study of Eastern Europe in the late sixteenth century, I read of a Cossack attack upon the apparently insignificant Crimean town of Gözlev (modern Russian Evpatoria) in 1589.[23] Nowhere in the Ottoman sources could I find any special reason for such an attack. Then I came across a *Zeitung,* describing the event in some detail, entitled *Vraye Relation de la Route . . . des Tartares* (Lyon, 1590), which had been circulated throughout Western Europe shortly after the event. According to the account, Gözlev, doubtless the principal seaport of the Crimean Khanate, had been holding a trade fair and the Cossacks, rightly expecting to find the streets and shops filled with finery and weapons, had timed their attack in accordance with the opening of the fair.

It is comparative work along these lines which can be so rewarding for the Islamic historian and it is within this context that my own researches have drawn me into the fascinating, but precarious, world of the *Zeitungen.* In summary, to use properly the vast store of information available in the *Zeitungen,* one must have a good idea of the development of the *genre* as well as the events which they describe. One is then in a position to evaluate any given item in relation to its centre of dissemination. Thereafter, where possible, one must go one step further and attempt to discover a document or some other more original source as corroboration, whether from a chancery, a renegade, a Papal nuncio, the *bailli* of Venice,

[23]S. M. Solov'ev, *Istoriya Rossii,* VII (Moscow, 1960), 261–262.

an Ottoman dragoman, a traveler, a court physician or even a "war correspondent," a person assigned to military units by governments and business houses as a *"Zeitungschreiber,"* who apparently first appeared in the Imperial wars of Eastern Europe at the close of the sixteenth century. Quite obviously also, when dealing with questions of the *Türkengefahr,* the editor or historian can well put to use the knowledge of Turkish, Russian, and other *"exotica"* from the East.[24]

[24]The late J. Sauvaget and R. Blachère produced a guide for editing and translating Arabic texts entitled *Règles pour éditions et traductions des textes arabes* (Paris, 1945) (Société d'édition "Les Belles lettres," Paris, 1945). For some interesting observations on the general impact of printing, see the recent study by K. Schottenloher, *Bücher Bewegten die Welt, Eine Kulturgeschichte des Buches,* 2 vols. (Stuttgart, 1952), especially II, pp. 321–5.

INDEX

This is, in the main, an index of names; but there has been no attempt to index the individual titles of plays for the first paper or individual titles of books published by Rouillé. Nor has there been any indexing of individual books and manuscripts at individual libraries for Professor Davis' paper. All name references have not been judged significant enough to be indexed.

ABERDEEN UNIVERSITY LIBRARY 83*n*, 104*ff*

Abrabanel, Judah 78*n*, 94*n*

Adams, J. Q. 13, 17

Aitzing, Michael von 123–4

d'Albenas, Jean Poldo 80*n*, 102*n*

Alberi, E. 117*n*

Alciati, A. 76*n*, *ff*, 92, 100*n*; see de las Brozas

Alexis of Piedmont 86, 89

Allen, P. S. 44*n*

Aneau, B. 80*n*, 91, 97, 99*n*, 101–2

Angers 4, 62

"Anonimus, Adam" 55

Anselm, Saint 64

Antwerp 35, 48, 54, 61, 72*ff*, 118

Aquinas, Thomas, Saint 62, 85*n*

Arabic, script, 126; texts, editing and translating, 129*n*

Arber, Edward 57*n*

Ariosto 29, 77, 87, 91, 103, 111

Aristotle 62

Armstrong, Elizabeth 77*n*, *ff*, 89*n*

Arnoullet, Balthazar 84*n*

Artour, Thomas 45

Ascarelli, F. 74*n*

Augsburg, 116*ff*

Augustine, Saint 64, 85*n*

BALD, R. C. 3, 9, 10–11, 17, 26*n*, 41

Balić, P. Carlo 42

Barker, Christopher 56

Basel 83

Baskervill, C. R. 13

Bassett, Mary 70

Baudrier, J. 72*ff*

Bawcutt, N. W. 14

Beaumont, Francis 12, 18

Benn, Ernest 16

Becke, Edmund 57–8

Berthelet, Thomas 46*ff*

Birley, Robert 7

Bizari, Pietro 80*n*

Blachère, 9. 129*n*

Boccaccio 77*ff*

Boleyn, Anne 44

———, Thomas 44, 51

Bond, R. W. 13

Bongi, S. 74*n*, 90*n*

Bonhomme, Macé 85*n*

Borrel, Jean 84*n*

Bourg, Marguérite de 87*n*

Bowers, Fredson 9, 18, 26*n*, 37*n*, 41; school of 16

Breslau 120

Bristol 61

Brockbank, Philip 15

Brooke, Tucker 13, 20–1

Brown, Arthur 23

Brown University Library 4, 80*ff*

de las Brozas, Francisco Sanchez 78*n*, 102*n*

Brucioli 90

Brückner, W. 119

Bullen, A. H. 18–19

Burnet, John 10–11

Byckman, F. *frontispiece*

Byddell, John 45, 50–1*ff*

CALVIN, JOHN 85
Cambis, Marguérite de 78*n*
Campana, Cesare 125
Canterbury 57
Cardano, Girolamo 110
Castiglione 77, 105
Catullus 39, 78*n*
Cawood, John 58, 61*ff*
Chaloner, Thomas 57
Chamard, Henri 28*ff*, 91*n*
Chapman, George 16*n*, 18, 25, 26*n*
Chapuys, E. 50
Charles V 50, 116, 118
Charles Emanuel, Duke of Savoy
　　89*n*
Charrière, E. 117*n*
Chaucer 23
Chauvet, Paul 75*n*
Church Fathers, the 84*ff*
Cicero 62, 78*ff*
Clair, Colin 74*n*
classics, editing of 5, 72*ff*
Clements, R. J. 91*n*, 92*n*
Cleveland Medical Library 84*n*
Cochlaeus, J. 64
Coldwell, C. S. 53*n*
Colet, John 50, 52, 64
collating 36*ff*
Cologne 120, 122
Columbia University Library 83*ff*
common places 101
computer 37
Constantin, Antoine 76*n*
Constantinople 80*n*
Contes de Vintemille, Jacques des
　　80*n*
Cop, Guillaume 83
Corpus juris civilis 82*ff*
Council of Trent 85*n*, 97, 110, 116
Coverdale, Myles 54, 56
Cox, Leonard 56
———, Thomas 51
Crasser, Jeremias 118

Cromwell, Gregory 51
Cromwell, Thomas 44*ff*, 59
Curtains Playwrights series 17

DALECHAMPS, JACQUES 83*ff*
Dante 77, 100, 102*n*
Daza, Bernardino 101*n*
Delcourt, Joseph 62
dépôt légal 34*ff*
Desportes, Philippe 28*ff*
de Roover, Raymond 74*n*
de Worde, Wynkyn 45, 50, 54
Dionysius the Areopagite 85*n*
Dioscorides 84
Dolet, Etienne 75*n*, 95
Domenichi, Lodovido 73*n*, *ff*
Donaldson, Ian 16*n*
Donat 89*n*
double-translation 46
Dowes, Henry 51
Droz, publishers 29
Droz, E. 82*n*
Du Bellay, J. 28*ff*, 91
Du Choul, Guillaume 73*n*, 82,
　　90*n*, 98*n*
Duaren, 89*n*
DuLin, Hélouin 95
Du Moulin, 82*n*
Durandus, commentaries 84*n*
Dürer, Albrecht 123*n*
Dyce, Alex. 19

ECKIUS, J. 64
Edward VI 55, 58, 59
Einblattdruck 114
Elyot, Sir Thomas 25
emblems, 92, 98, 101*ff* (see also
　　Alciati, Praz
Entrata 80*n*
Erasmus 43*ff*, 60*ff*; editions of
　　Church Fathers 54; Erasmian
　　Catholics 95; projected editions
　　of 4; translations 43*ff*
d'Este, Ippolito 95*n*
Estienne, Henri 120

——, Robert 33, 72*ff*, 89*n*
Eskrich, Pierre 102
Everard, N. 111
Evpatoria, *see* Gözlev

FABER, J. 64
Farmer, reprint 19
Febvre, L. 73*n*
Ferdinand II 125
Ferguson, W. K. 51*n*
Ffoakes, R. A. 14
Ferus, J. 84
Ficino, Marsilio 78*n*
Fischer-Galati, Stephen 115*n*
Fisher, John 64
Fitzler, M. A. H. 118*n*
Fletcher, John 12, 18
Flugschriften 114*ff*
Folger Library 78*ff*
Fowler, John 61–2, 64
Foxe, John 45
Frankfurt 72*ff*, 113*ff*, 119*ff*
Frankus, Jacobus 124
French Academie, The 25
Fuchs, Leonhard 105
Fugger, house of, 118; newsletters 118, 122

GABIANO, L. de 75, 77*n*
Galen 83, 88, 100
Gardiner, Stephen 56
gazzetta 117*n*
Gee, J. A. 46*n*
Geneva 103
Gerrard, Philip 55
Gibson, R. W. 60*ff*
Gilles, Pierre 80*n*
Gilmore, Myron P. 82*n*
Giolito, Giovanni and Gabriello 74*ff*
giornale 117*n*
Giovio, Paolo 78, 81*n*, 91*n*, 98, 103
Giuntini, Francesco 90*n*
Goldschmidt, E. P. 7
Göllner, C. 119*n*
Gough, John 54

Gözlev 128
Grafton, Richard 54*ff*
Graham, Howard Jay 6*n*
Graham, Victor E. 94*n*
Grande Compagnie des Libraires 75*ff*
Greene, Robert 13, 15, 18; Collins' edition of, 13
Greg, W. W. 21*n*, 41
Groulleau, Etienne 76*n*
Gryphius, S. 72*ff*
Guevara 78*n*
Gülfferich, H. 121*n*

HAMBURG 120
Harbage, Alfred 18
Harrier, Richard 21
Harris, John 62
Harvard University—Houghton Library 78*ff*
Hastings, Margaret 9
Hauser, H. 75*n*
Havet, E. 42
Henri II 80*n*, 89*n*
Henry VIII 50*ff*, 59, 97
Herodianus 78
Hervet, Gentian 46
Heywood, John 12, 18
——, Thomas 12, 18
Heyworth, Peter L. 3
Hippocrates 78*n*, 83, 88–9
Hoeniger, F. D. 23
Hohenemser, P. 119*n*
Holmes, Catherine 83*n*
Hoochstraten, Johannes 47–8
Horace 78*n*, 99, 101, 110
Horder, M. 121*n*
Hosius, Stanislaus 97
Hosley, Richard 18
Hotman, F. 82*n*
Houghton Library, *see* Harvard
Houlier, Jacques 83*n*, 89*n*
Hoy, Cyrus 15–16, 18, 22, 26*n*
Huguet 40
Hyrde, Richard 45

IACOT, DESIDERÉ 83*n*, 88*n*
Indexes of Prohibited Books 85, 97, 110
Innis, H. A. 123*n*
Islamic studies 127
Istvanfi, Nicolas 125
Italian printing 5, 72*ff*

JEROME, SAINT 63
Johnson, W. McAllister 95*n*
Jonas, Jodocus 50
Jonson, Ben 25; Herford and Simpson edition 13
Julius II 50–1

KEY, THOMAS 55
Khevenhüller, Graf Franz Christoph 125
Kingdon, Robert 74*n*, 88–9
Kisch, Guido 82*n*
Klarwill, Victor von 118*n*
Kling, Melchior 111
Kluge, F. 113*n*
Kertbény, K. M. 119*n*
Knolles, Richard 124, 126

LAMBARDE, WILLIAM 6*n*
Lambert, John 53
Lambin, Denis 78*n*
Lepanto 115
Lapeyre, H. 87*n*
La Porte 75*n*
La Tayssonière, Guillaume de 77*n*
Laumonier, Paul 28*ff*
Lautenbach, *see* Frankus, Jacobus
Lavaud, Jacques 28*ff*
LaVille, Claude 76*n*
LeClercq, J. 44*n*
Lefèvre d'Étaples 85*n*
legal books 81*ff*
Leonicus, Nicolaus 83
Lesse, Nicholas 57
Leucht, Valentin 119*n*
libraire 34*ff*, 77*ff*

Liddell, Duncan 83*n*
Linacre, T. 83
Liotard, Pierre 35*n*
loci communes, see common places
Lombard, P. 84*n*
Lordi, R. J. 26*n*
Louis XII 91
Lübeck 120
Luft, Hans, *see* Hoochstraten
Luther, Martin 64, 96, 115–16, 119, 121; his printer 47
Lyly, John 13, 15, 18
Lyon 31*ff*, 72*ff*, 122, 128
Lyre, Nicolas de 63*ff*, 85*n*

MCCONICA, JAMES K. 8*n*, 49
McKerrow, R. B. 9
McLuhan, H. M. 113 & *n*
Mainz 85, 119
Malherbe, François de 33*ff*
Malet, Francis 55
Malone Society 42
Manutius, Aldus 78, 88
Marburg 47
Marguérite de France, Duchess of Berry 89*n*
Marlowe, Christopher 14, 18–19, 20–1, 25
Marot, Clément 77*ff*, 91, 100–1
Marshall, William 50, 53
Marston, John 15, 18–19
Martin, H. J. 73*n*
Martz, Louis L. 64–5
Mary, Queen of England 58, 60*ff*
Massinger, Phillip 12, 15, 18
mathematics, books on 84, 93
Matthioli, P. A. 84, 89*n*, 93
Medici, Catherine de 89
medicine, books on 81*ff*
Medina del Campo 72
Melancthon, Phillipp 119
Mercklin, Balthasar 53
Mermaid editions 13*ff*, 25
Mess-relationen 123

Meurerius, T. 124
Meyer, Bruno 41
Michigan, University of, Library 78*ff*
Middleton, Thomas 12, 14–15, 18; and Rowley 14
Mirandola, Pico della 64
Mirror for Magistrates, The 25
Modern Language Association 12, 16
Mohács 114*ff*
Monmouth, Humphrey 45
Montréal, Université de 88*n*
Montreux, Nicolas de 125
More, Sir Thomas (Saint); daughter, 44, 46; prayer-book of, frontispiece; Valencia holograph, 69; works of, 8*ff*
Morison, Richard 54
Morize, André 41
Mortimer, Ruth 72*ff*, 99*n*
"mos gallicus" 82
"mos italicus" 82
Moulins, Jean des 84*n*, 93*n*
Mountjoy, William Blount, Lord 49
music, printing of 92
Mychell, John 57
mythology 39

NAPLES 72
Navaro, Martin Azpilcueta 87, 102*n*
Navaro, Martin Azpilcueta 87, 102*n*
Navarre, Marguérite de 77*n*
Négociations 117*ff*
New Arden series 14, 21
Newberry Library 73*ff*
New Mermaid series 15
New York Academy of Medicine 83*n*
New York Public Library 78*ff*
New York, Union Theological Seminary 84*n*
Nicolay, Nicolas de 80, 86*n*, 103*n*

Nouvellen 118
Nürnberg 117*ff*

ONG, WALTER J., S.J. 100–1
Ornstein, Robert 17–18
Ortelius, A. 125
Ovid 39, 91*n*
Oxford Bibliographical Society 43

PAPER 73 & *n*
Paris 35*ff*, 73*ff*
Parr, Catherine 54*ff*
Parrish, S. M. 37
Parry, V. J. 113, 124*n*
Paterno, 78*ff*
Patrick, J. Max 21
Payen, Thibaud 75*n*, 76–7
Paynell, Thomas 54, 61*ff*
Peele, George 19
Peletier, Jacques 91–2
Pelicanus, Conradus, Epistle to 58
Perez, Hernan 98*n*
Périers, Bonaventure de 77*n*
Petrarch 39, 77, 87, 91, 100*ff*
Phillip II 116
Pillet, Vincent 75*n*
Pinet, Antoine du 84*n*
plaidoyers 83
Plantin, Christophe 74*ff*
Pléiade, the 72*ff*, 91*ff*
Plucknett, T. F. T. 6*n*
Pole, Margaret, Countess of Salisbury 46
Pontoux, Claude de 102
Porter, Henry 15
Portunariis, Vincent de 76*ff*
Praz, Mario 92*n*
privilège 34*ff*
proof-reading 37, 98
Psalms 34, 85*ff*
Ptolemy 120*n*

RAMUS, P. 100–1
Rastell, William 8, 60*ff*
Rath, P. 121*n*

Redman, Robert 54
Reed, A. W. 46*n*
Reformers (English) 4
Regents Renaissance Drama series 15*ff*, 21, 24
Regnault, F. *frontispiece*
relationes 114 *ff*
Reusch, H. 85*n*, 97*n*
Revels Plays series 14*ff*, 24
Rhenanus, Beatus 64
Ribner, Irving 18*ff*
Ricci, Agostino 83*n*
Rice, Eugene F. 85*n*
Riddell, William 58
Ridolfi, Luca Antonio 78*ff*, 90, 99*n*, 102
Ronsard, Pierre de 28
Rochemore, Jacques de 78*n*
Roman law 82*ff*
Rondelet, Guillaume 83*n*, 89*n*, 98–9, 111
Roper Margaret 44*ff*, 64
Roper, Margaret 44*ff*, 64
Rouen 35
Rouillé, Guillaume 72*ff*
———, Mathieu 76
———, Philippe Gautier 76*n*, 78*n*
Rudler, Gustave 29, 41
Ruscelli, I. 111

SACHS, HANS 123*n*
Saconay, Gabriel de 97
St. German, Christopher 6*n*
Saragossa 72
Sauvage, Denis 78*n* & *ff*
Sauvaget, J. 129*n*
Schiffle, Jeremias 118
Schottenloher, Karl 115*n*, 119*n*, 129*n*
science, books in 84
Seguin, J.-P. 121*n*
Senneton (*printing family of Lyon*) 75*n*
Shakespeare, 14*ff*, 25; Globe ed. 17; *Merchant of Venice* 117; New

Arden series 14; Pelican ed. 18
Shirley, James 12, 15, 18
Sibmacher, Johannes 125
Simeoni, Gabriello 77, 90*n*, 98, 108
Somerset, Edward Seymour, Duke of 56
Sonnius 97*n*
Spelling, old *vs.* modern 21*ff*, 38*ff*
Spencer, Hazelton 13, 18
Spenser, E. 23
Stafford, Henry Lord 58
Staverton, Frances 46
Stevens, Linton C. 82*n*
Strassburg 120
Strype, John 58
Sullivan, Frank 8
Sylvester, Richard S. 7*ff*
Sylvius, J. 83

TAGAULT, JEAN 84, 88, 108
Taverner, Richard 48–9, 54
Taylor, Robert H. 7*n*
Termes, Madame de 87*n*
Theophrastus 84
Thompson, Craig R. 58*n*
Thompson, James W. 120*n*
Thorne, Samuel E. 6*n*
Tinghi, Baccio 90*n*
———, Philippe 76*n*
Tiraqueau, André 110
Titelmann, Fr. 85, 100*n*, 106*ff*
Toronto Academy of Medicine 83*n*
Toronto Public Library 7, 78*ff*
Toronto, University of, Library 78*ff*; Press 37
Tottell, Richard 60*ff*
Tournes, Jean de 72*ff*
Tourneur, Cyril 14
Toy, John 51
troubadours 39
Türkengefahr 115
Turks 80, 113*ff*
Tyard, Pontus de 91*n*
Tyndale, William 44*ff*
Tyndall, Martin 50

UDALL, NICHOLAS 54*ff*
Union Catalogue (Washington) 31
Urrea 103*n*

VAGANAY, HUGUES 31*ff*
Vaughan, D. M. 115*n*
Venice 72*ff*, 116*ff*, 121, 125
Vienna 114*ff*
Vincent (printing family of Lyon) 75*n*
Vintemille, Jacques de 91*n*
Vitrier, John 50
Volzius, Paul 45

WALEY, JOHN 61*ff*
Walsh, Sir John and Lady 44
Wayland, John 52
Webster, John 13, 25; Lucas edition 13
Weinberg, Bernard 91*n*, 99*n*, 101*n*

Wellcome Historical Medical Library (London) 104*ff*
Wells, James 74*n*
Whitchurch, Edward 56
White, Helen C. 53*n*
Whittington, Robert 54
Wightman, W. P. D. 83*n*, 104*n*
Wittenberg 119, 121
Wittkower, Rudolf 95*n*
Wolsey, Cardinal 48
Worms, Diet of 116
Wycliffe, John 63
Wyer, Robert 54

YALE EDITION OF MORE 4, 7*ff*
Yates, Frances A. 90*n*, 92*n*

ZASIUS, U. 82*n*
Zeitung 113*ff*
Zeitungschreiber 129